COLLECT
BRITISH
STAMPS

A STANLEY GIBBONS CHECKLIST OF
THE STAMPS OF GREAT BRITAIN

Forty-second Edition

STANLEY GIBBONS PUBLICATIONS LTD
By Appointment to H. M. the Queen
Stanley Gibbons Ltd, London Philatelists.

London and Ringwood

COLLECT BRITISH STAMPS

The 42nd Edition

From the famous Penny Black of 1840 to the absorbing issues of today, the stamps of Great Britain are highly popular with collectors. *Collect British Stamps* has been our message since very early days – but particularly since the First Edition of this checklist in September 1967. This 42nd edition includes all the recent issues. Prices have been carefully revised to reflect today's market. Total sales of *Collect British Stamps* are now over 3¼ million copies.

Collect British Stamps appears in the autumn of each year. A more detailed Great Britain catalogue, the *Concise*, is published each spring. The *Great Britain Concise* incorporates many additional listings covering watermark varieties, phosphor omitted errors, missing colour errors, stamp booklets and special commemorative First Day Cover postmarks. It is ideally suited for the collector who wishes to discover more about GB stamps.

Listings in this edition of *Collect British Stamps* include all 1990 issues which have appeared up to the publication date.

Scope. *Collect British Stamps* comprises:
- All stamps with different watermark (*wmk*) or perforation (*perf*).
- Visible plate numbers on the Victorian issues.
- Graphite-lined and phosphor issues, including variations in the number of phosphor bands.
- First Day Covers for all Special Issues.
- Special Sections for Definitive and Regional First Day Covers of the present reign.
- Presentation, Gift and Souvenir Packs.
- Post Office Yearbooks.
- Regional issues and War Occupation stamps of Guernsey and Jersey.
- Postage Due and Official Stamps.
- Post Office Picture Cards (PHQ cards).
- Commemorative gutter pairs and "Traffic Light" gutter pairs listed as mint sets.
- Royal Mail Postage Labels priced as sets and on P.O. First Day Cover.

Stamps of the independent postal administrations of Guernsey, Isle of Man and Jersey are contained in *Collect Channel Islands and Isle of Man Stamps*.

Layout. Stamps are set out chronologically by date of issue. In the catalogue lists the first numeral is the Stanley Gibbons catalogue number; the black (boldface) numeral alongside is the type number referring to the respective illustration. A blank in this column implies that the number immediately above is repeated. The denomination and colour of the stamp are then shown. Before February 1971 British currency was:

£1=20s	One pound=twenty shillings *and*
1s=12d	One shilling=twelve pence.

Upon decimalisation this became:

£1=100p	One pound=one hundred (new) pence.

The catalogue list then shows two price columns. The left-hand is for unused stamps and the right-hand for used. Corresponding small boxes are provided in which collectors may wish to check off the items in their collection.

Our method of indicating prices is:
Numerals for pence, e.g. 5 denotes 5p (5 pence)
Numerals for pounds and pence, e.g. 4·25 denotes £4·25 (4 pounds and 25 pence).
For £100 and above, prices are in whole pounds and so include the £ sign and omit the zeros for pence.

Colour illustrations. The colour illustrations of stamps are intended as a guide only; they may differ in shade from the originals.

Size of illustrations. To comply with Post Office regulations stamp illustrations are three-quarters linear size. Separate illustrations of surcharges, overprints and watermarks are actual size.

Prices. Prices quoted in this catalogue are our selling prices at the time the book went to press. They are for stamps in fine condition; in issues where condition varies we may ask more for the superb and less for the sub-standard. The unused prices for stamps of Queen Victoria to King Edward VIII are for lightly hinged examples. Unused prices for King George VI and Queen Elizabeth II are for unmounted mint (though when not available unmounted, mounted stamps are often supplied at a lower price). Prices for used stamps refer to postally used copies. All prices are subject to change without prior notice and we give no guarantee to supply all stamps priced, since it is not possible to keep every catalogued item in stock. Commemorative issues may, at times, only be available in complete sets and not as individual values.

In the price columns:
= Does not exist.
—) or blank = Exists, or may exist, but price cannot be quoted.
= Not normally issued (the so-called 'Abnormals' of 1862–80).

Perforations. The 'perforation' is the number of holes in a length of 2 cm, as measured by the Gibbons *Instanta* gauge. The stamp is viewed against a dark background with the transparent gauge put on top of it. Perforations are quoted to the nearest half. Stamps without perforation are termed 'imperforate'.

Se-tenant block

Se-tenant combinations. *Se-tenant* means 'joined together'. Some sets include stamps of different design arranged *se-tenant* as blocks or strips and these are often collected unsevered as issued. Where such combinations exist the stamps are priced both mint and used, as singles or complete combinations. The set price for mint refers to the unsevered combination plus singles of any other values in the set. The used set price is for single stamps of all values.

First day covers. Prices for first day covers are for complete sets used on plain covers (1924, 1925, 1929) or on special covers (1935 onwards), the stamps of which are cancelled with ordinary operational postmarks (1924–1962) or by the *standard* "First Day of Issue" postmarks (1963 onwards). Where the stamps in a set were issued on different days, prices are for a cover from each day.

PHQ cards. Since 1973 the Post Office has produced a series of picture cards, which can be sent through the post as postcards. Each card shows an enlarged colour reproduction of a current British stamp, either of one or more values from a set or of all values. Cards are priced here in fine mint condition for sets complete as issued. The Post Office gives each card a 'PHQ' serial number, hence the term. The cards are usually on sale shortly before the date of issue of the stamps, but there is no officially designated 'first day'.

Used prices are for cards franked with the stamp depicted, on the obverse or reverse; the stamp being cancelled with an official postmark for first day of issue.

Gutter pairs. All modern Great Britain commemoratives are produced in sheets containing two panes of stamps separated by a blank horizontal or vertical margin known as a gutter. This feature first made its appearance on some supplies of the 1972 Royal Silver Wedding 3p, and marked the introduction of Harrison & Sons' new "Jumelle" stamp-printing press. There are advantages for both the printer and the Post

Office in such a layout which has now been used for all commemorative issues since 1974.

The term "gutter pair" is used for a pair of stamps separated by part of the blank gutter margin.

Gutter pair

Most printers include some form of colour check device on the sheet margins, in addition to the cylinder or plate numbers. Harrison & Sons use round "dabs", or spots of colour, resembling traffic lights. For the period from the 1972 Royal Silver Wedding until the end of 1979 these colour dabs appeared in the gutter margin. Gutter pairs showing these "traffic lights" are worth considerably more than the normal version.

Traffic light gutter pair

Catalogue numbers used. The checklist uses the same catalogue numbers as the Stanley Gibbons *British Commonwealth* Catalogue (Part 1), 1991 edition.

Latest issue date for stamps recorded in this edition is 13 November 1990.

STANLEY GIBBONS LTD

Head Office: 399 Strand, London WC2R 0LX. Auction Room and Specialist Stamp Departments—Open Monday-Friday 9.30 a.m to 5 p.m.
Shop—Open Monday–Friday 9.30 a.m. to 6.00 p.m. and Saturday 10 a.m. to 4 p.m.

Telephone 071-836 8444 and Telex 28883 for all departments

Stanley Gibbons Publications Ltd:
Editorial, Sales Offices and
Distribution Centre,
5, Parkside, Christchurch Road,
Ringwood, Hants BH24 3SH.
Telephone 0425 472363

ISBN: 0-85259-277-9
© Stanley Gibbons Publications Ltd 1990

QUEEN VICTORIA

1837 (20 June)–1901 (22 Jan.)

IDENTIFICATION. In this checklist Victorian stamps are classified firstly according to which printing method was used – line-engraving, embossing or surface-printing.

Corner letters. Numerous stamps also have letters in all four, or just the lower, corners. These were an anti-forgery device and the letters differ from stamp to stamp. If present in all four corners the upper pair are the reverse of the lower. Note the importance of these corner letters in the way the checklist is arranged.

Watermarks. Further classification depends on watermarks: these are illustrated in normal position, with stamps priced accordingly.

1 Line-engraved Issues

1

1a

2

2a White lines added above and below head

3 Small Crown watermark

4 Large Crown watermark

Letters in lower corners

1840 *Wmk Small Crown Type* **3** *Imperforate*

Cat. No.	Type			Unused	Used		
2	1	1d black	.. ..	£2750	£140	☐	☐
5	2	2d blue	.. ..	£5500	£300	☐	☐

1841

8	1a	1d red-brown	..	£125	3·00	☐	☐
14	2a	2d blue	.. ..	£1000	35·00	☐	☐

1854–57 *(i) Wmk Small Crown Type* **3** *Perf* 16

17	1a	1d red-brown	..	£120	3·00	☐	☐
19	2a	2d blue	.. ..	£1250	35·00	☐	☐

(ii) Wmk Small Crown Type **3** *Perf* 14

24	1a	1d red-brown	..	£225	15·00	☐	☐
23a	2a	2d blue	.. ..	£1750	£110	☐	☐

(iii) Wmk Large Crown Type **4** *Perf* 16

26	1a	1d red	.. .. ..	£400	28·00	☐	☐
27	2a	2d blue	.. ..	£2000	£125	☐	☐

(iv) Wmk Large Crown Type **4** *Perf* 14

40	1a	1d red	.. .. ..	25·00	60	☐	☐
34	2a	2d blue	.. ..	£1000	25·00	☐	☐

5

6 Watermark extending over three stamps

7

8

9

Letters in all four corners

Plate numbers. Stamps included a 'plate number' in their design and this affects valuation. The cheapest plates are priced here; see complete list of plate numbers overleaf.

1858–70 *(i) Wmk Type* **6** *Perf* 14

48	5	½d red	.. ..	40·00	5·00	☐	☐

(ii) Wmk Large Crown Type **4** *Perf* 14

43	7	1d red	.. .. ..	9·00	60	☐	☐
51	8	1½d red	.. ..	£150	16·00	☐	☐
45	9	2d blue	.. ..	£150	2·50	☐	☐

PLATE NUMBERS
on stamps of 1858–70 having letters in all four corners

Positions of Plate Numbers

Shows
Plate 9 (½d)

Shows
Plate 170 (1d. 2d)

Shows
Plate 3 (1½d)

HALFPENNY VALUE (S.G. 48)

Plate	Un.	Used			Plate	Un.	Used		
1	90·00	35·00	☐	☐	11	40·00	5·00	☐	☐
3	55·00	14·00	☐	☐	12	40·00	5·00	☐	☐
4	70·00	7·00	☐	☐	13	40·00	5·00	☐	☐
5	50·00	5·00	☐	☐	14	40·00	5·00	☐	☐
6	40·00	5·00	☐	☐	15	55·00	9·00	☐	☐
8	80·00	35·00	☐	☐	19	85·00	18·00	☐	☐
9	£2000	£300	☐	☐	20	90·00	30·00	☐	☐
10	70·00	5·00	☐	☐					

Plates 2, 7, 16, 17 and 18 were not completed, while Plates 21 and 22, though made, were not used. Plate 9 was a reserve plate, not greatly used.

PENNY VALUE (S.G. 43)

Plate	Un.	Used			Plate	Un.	Used			Plate	Un.	Used			Plate	Un.	Used		
71	22·00	3·00	☐	☐	112	60·00	1·50	☐	☐	154	15·00	60	☐	☐	190	10·00	5·00	☐	☐
72	35·00	3·50	☐	☐	113	15·00	11·00	☐	☐	155	16·00	1·00	☐	☐	191	9·00	6·00	☐	☐
73	25·00	3·00	☐	☐	114	£350	12·00	☐	☐	156	15·00	75	☐	☐	192	25·00	75	☐	☐
74	20·00	75	☐	☐	115	£100	1·50	☐	☐	157	15·00	75	☐	☐	193	9·00	75	☐	☐
76	40·00	75	☐	☐	116	75·00	9·00	☐	☐	158	9·00	75	☐	☐	194	15·00	7·00	☐	☐
77	£50000	£30000	☐	☐	117	16·00	60	☐	☐	159	9·00	75	☐	☐	195	15·00	7·00	☐	☐
78	£100	75	☐	☐	118	25·00	75	☐	☐	160	9·00	60	☐	☐	196	10·00	4·00	☐	☐
79	30·00	60	☐	☐	119	10·00	1·00	☐	☐	161	29·00	6·00	☐	☐	197	16·00	12·00	☐	☐
80	20·00	1·25	☐	☐	120	9·00	60	☐	☐	162	16·00	6·00	☐	☐	198	9·00	5·00	☐	☐
81	60·00	1·50	☐	☐	121	40·00	9·00	☐	☐	163	15·00	2·00	☐	☐	199	20·00	5·00	☐	☐
82	£120	3·50	☐	☐	122	9·00	60	☐	☐	164	15·00	3·00	☐	☐	200	20·00	75	☐	☐
83	£140	6·00	☐	☐	123	12·00	1·00	☐	☐	165	20·00	75	☐	☐	201	9·00	6·00	☐	☐
84	60·00	1·50	☐	☐	124	12·00	60	☐	☐	166	15·00	5·00	☐	☐	202	15·00	7·00	☐	☐
85	25·00	1·50	☐	☐	125	15·00	2·00	☐	☐	167	10·00	70	☐	☐	203	9·00	15·00	☐	☐
86	30·00	3·50	☐	☐	127	35·00	2·00	☐	☐	168	12·00	7·00	☐	☐	204	12·00	1·00	☐	☐
87	9·00	1·00	☐	☐	129	11·00	7·00	☐	☐	169	30·00	6·00	☐	☐	205	11·00	3·00	☐	☐
88	£160	8·00	☐	☐	130	18·00	1·50	☐	☐	170	11·00	60	☐	☐	206	11·00	11·00	☐	☐
89	40·00	75	☐	☐	131	75·00	16·00	☐	☐	171	9·00	60	☐	☐	207	12·00	12·00	☐	☐
90	28·00	75	☐	☐	132	£100	24·00	☐	☐	172	9·00	1·25	☐	☐	208	11·00	15·00	☐	☐
91	40·00	5·00	☐	☐	133	90·00	9·00	☐	☐	173	50·00	9·00	☐	☐	209	15·00	12·00	☐	☐
92	15·00	75	☐	☐	134	9·00	60	☐	☐	174	9·00	60	☐	☐	210	20·00	18·00	☐	☐
93	40·00	75	☐	☐	135	£100	30·00	☐	☐	175	35·00	2·50	☐	☐	211	42·00	25·00	☐	☐
94	40·00	4·00	☐	☐	136	£100	20·00	☐	☐	176	25·00	1·25	☐	☐	212	15·00	15·00	☐	☐
95	25·00	75	☐	☐	137	15·00	1·25	☐	☐	177	10·00	75	☐	☐	213	15·00	15·00	☐	☐
96	28·00	60	☐	☐	138	9·00	60	☐	☐	178	15·00	3·00	☐	☐	214	25·00	25·00	☐	☐
97	15·00	2·50	☐	☐	139	20·00	16·00	☐	☐	179	16·00	1·50	☐	☐	215	25·00	25·00	☐	☐
98	15·00	5·00	☐	☐	140	9·00	60	☐	☐	180	16·00	4·00	☐	☐	216	25·00	25·00	☐	☐
99	25·00	4·00	☐	☐	141	£150	9·00	☐	☐	181	15·00	75	☐	☐	217	15·00	5·00	☐	☐
100	35·00	1·75	☐	☐	142	50·00	25·00	☐	☐	182	£100	4·00	☐	☐	218	11·00	7·00	☐	☐
101	50·00	8·00	☐	☐	143	30·00	15·00	☐	☐	183	25·00	2·00	☐	☐	219	60·00	75·00	☐	☐
102	20·00	80	☐	☐	144	£100	20·00	☐	☐	184	9·00	1·00	☐	☐	220	9·00	7·00	☐	☐
103	19·00	2·00	☐	☐	145	9·00	1·50	☐	☐	185	15·00	2·00	☐	☐	221	29·00	20·00	☐	☐
104	28·00	4·00	☐	☐	146	10·00	5·00	☐	☐	186	30·00	1·50	☐	☐	222	35·00	40·00	☐	☐
105	65·00	6·00	☐	☐	147	18·00	3·00	☐	☐	187	11·00	75	☐	☐	223	50·00	70·00	☐	☐
106	30·00	80	☐	☐	148	20·00	2·50	☐	☐	188	20·00	10·00	☐	☐	224	65·00	65·00	☐	☐
107	40·00	5·50	☐	☐	149	15·00	5·00	☐	☐	189	35·00	6·00	☐	☐	225	£1500	£400	☐	☐
108	30·00	1·50	☐	☐	150	9·00	60	☐	☐										
109	75·00	2·50	☐	☐	151	25·00	9·00	☐	☐										
110	19·00	8·00	☐	☐	152	18·00	4·50	☐	☐										
111	35·00	1·50	☐	☐	153	70·00	8·00	☐	☐										

Plates 69, 70, 75, 77, 126 and 128 were prepared but rejected. No stamps therefore exist, except for a very few from Plate 77 which somehow reached the public. Plate 177 stamps, by accident or design, are sometimes passed off as the rare Plate 77.

THREE-HALFPENNY VALUE (S.G. 51)

Plate	Un.	Used			Plate	Un.	Used		
(1)	£350	20·00	☐	☐	3	£150	16·00	☐	☐

Plate 1 did not have the plate number in the design. Plate 2 was not completed and no stamps exist.

TWOPENNY VALUE (S.G. 45)

Plate	Un.	Used			Plate	Un.	Used		
7	£400	15·00	☐	☐	13	£175	5·50	☐	☐
8	£450	11·00	☐	☐	14	£200	7·50	☐	☐
9	£150	2·50	☐	☐	15	£150	7·50	☐	☐
12	£700	40·00	☐	☐					

Plates 10 and 11 were prepared but rejected.

2 Embossed Issues

Prices are for stamps cut square and with average to fine embossing. Stamps with exceptionally clear embossing are worth more.

10

11

12

13

1847–54	Wmk 13 (6d), no wmk (others)		Imperforate			
59	10	6d lilac ..	.. ..	£2500	£375	☐ ☐
57	11	10d brown	.. ..	£2250	£550	☐ ☐
54	12	1s green	.. ..	£2750	£350	☐ ☐

3 Surface-printed Issues

IDENTIFICATION. Check first whether the design includes corner letters or not, as mentioned for 'Line-engraved issues'. The checklist is divided up according to whether any letters are small or large, also whether they are white (uncoloured) or printed in the colour of the stamp. Further identification then depends on watermark.

PERFORATION. Except for Nos. 126/9 all the following issues of Queen Victoria are perf 14.

14

15 Small Garter

16 Medium Garter

17 Large Garter

18

19

20 Emblems

No corner letters

1855–57 (i) Wmk Small Garter Type 15						
62	14	4d red ..	.. ..	£2250	£150	☐ ☐
(ii) Wmk Medium Garter Type 16						
64	14	4d red ..	.. ..	£1750	£130	☐ ☐
(iii) Wmk Large Garter Type 17						
66a	14	4d red ..	.. ..	£600	35·00	☐ ☐
(iv) Wmk Emblems Type 20						
70	18	6d lilac ..	.. ..	£500	35·00	☐ ☐
72	19	1s green	.. ..	£600	£100	☐ ☐

Plate numbers. Stamps Nos. 90/163 should be checked for the 'plate numbers' indicated, as this affects valuation (the cheapest plates are priced here). The mark '*Pl.*' shows that several numbers exist, priced in a separate list overleaf.

Plate numbers are the small numerals appearing in duplicate in some part of the frame design or adjacent to the lower corner letters (in the 5s value a single numeral above the lower inscription).

21

22

23

24

25

Small white corner letters

1862–64 Wmk Emblems Type 20, except 4d (Large Garter Type 17)						
77	21	3d red ..	.. ..	£700	95·00	☐ ☐
80	22	4d red ..	.. ..	£500	30·00	☐ ☐
84	23	6d lilac ..	.. ..	£650	28·00	☐ ☐
87	24	9d bistre	.. ..	£1100	£130	☐ ☐
90	25	1s green *Pl.* ..	.. ..	£700	60·00	☐ ☐

26

27

28 (hyphen in SIX-PENCE)

32

33 Spray of Rose

34

29

30

31

Large white corner letters

1865–67 *Wmk Emblems Type* **20**, *except 4d (Large Garter Type* **17**)

92	**26**	3d red (Plate 4) ..	£375	35·00	☐ ☐
94	**27**	4d vermilion *Pl.* ..	£225	15·00	☐ ☐
97	**28**	6d lilac *Pl.*	£350	28·00	☐ ☐
98	**29**	9d straw *Pl.*	£700	£170	☐ ☐
99	**30**	10d brown (Plate 1)	†	£12000	☐
101	**31**	1s green (Plate 4)	£650	60·00	☐ ☐

1867–80 *Wmk Spray of Rose Type* **33**

103	**26**	3d red *Pl.*	£200	12·00	☐
105	**28**	6d lilac (with hyphen) (Plate 6)	£550	28·00	☐
109		6d mauve (without hyphen) *Pl.* ..	£275	25·00	☐
111	**29**	9d straw (Plate 4)	£600	90·00	☐
112	**30**	10d brown *Pl.* ..	£1000	£120	☐
117	**31**	1s green *Pl.*	£350	10·00	☐
119	**32**	2s blue *Pl.*	£950	55·00	☐
121		2s brown (Plate 1)	£6000	£900	☐

1872–73 *Wmk Spray of Rose Type* **33**

123	**34**	6d brown *Pl.* ..	£350	18·00	☐
125		6d grey (Plate 12)	£600	70·00	☐

PLATE NUMBERS
on stamps
of 1862–83

Cat. No.		Plate No.	Un.	Used	
Small White Corner Letters (1862–64)					
90	1s green	2	£700	60·00	☐ ☐
		3	£11000		☐ ☐

Plate 2 is actually numbered as '1' and Plate 3 as '2' on the stamps.

Cat. No.		Plate No.	Un.	Used	
Large White Corner Letters (1865–83)					
103	3d red	4	£300	50·00	☐ ☐
		5	£200	14·00	☐ ☐
		6	£225	12·00	☐ ☐
		7	£275	15·00	☐ ☐
		8	£250	14·00	☐ ☐
		9	£250	18·00	☐ ☐
		10	£275	40·00	☐ ☐
94	4d verm	7	£300	19·00	☐ ☐
		8	£250	19·00	☐ ☐
		9	£250	15·00	☐ ☐
		10	£300	26·00	☐ ☐
		11	£250	15·00	☐ ☐
		12	£225	15·00	☐ ☐
		13	£250	17·00	☐ ☐
		14	£300	30·00	☐ ☐
97	6d lilac	5	£350	28·00	☐ ☐
		6	£1000	55·00	☐ ☐
109	6d mauve	8	£275	25·00	☐ ☐
		9	£275	25·00	☐ ☐
		10	*	£12000	☐ ☐
123	6d brown	11	£350	18·00	☐ ☐
		12	£750	50·00	☐ ☐

Cat. No.		Plate No.	Un.	Used	
98	9d straw	4	£700	£170	☐ ☐
		5	£10000	*	☐ ☐
112	10d brown	1	£1000	£120	☐ ☐
		2	£12000	£2500	☐ ☐
117	1s green	4	£350	15·00	☐ ☐
		5	£400	12·00	☐ ☐
		6	£525	10·00	☐ ☐
		7	£525	25·00	☐ ☐
119	2s blue	1	£950	55·00	☐ ☐
		3	*	£3000	☐ ☐
126	5s red	1	£2500	£250	☐ ☐
		2	£3500	£325	☐ ☐
Large Coloured Corner Letters (1873–83)					
139	2½d mauve	1	£225	25·00	☐ ☐
		2	£225	25·00	☐ ☐
		3	£400	30·00	☐ ☐
141	2½d mauve	3	£500	30·00	☐ ☐
		4	£200	12·00	☐ ☐
		5	£200	16·00	☐ ☐
		6	£200	12·00	☐ ☐
		7	£200	12·00	☐ ☐
		8	£200	16·00	☐ ☐
		9	£200	12·00	☐ ☐
		10	£225	17·00	☐ ☐
		11	£200	12·00	☐ ☐
		12	£200	16·00	☐ ☐
		13	£200	16·00	☐ ☐
		14	£200	12·00	☐ ☐
		15	£200	12·00	☐ ☐
		16	£200	12·00	☐ ☐
		17	£550	80·00	☐ ☐
142	2½d blue	17	£175	20·00	☐ ☐
		18	£200	12·00	☐ ☐
		19	£175	10·00	☐ ☐
		20	£175	10·00	☐ ☐

Cat. No.		Plate No.	Un.	Used	
157	2½d blue	21	£225	9·00	☐ ☐
		22	£175	8·00	☐ ☐
		23	£175	8·00	☐ ☐
143	3d red	11	£200	12·00	☐ ☐
		12	£225	14·00	☐ ☐
		14	£250	15·00	☐ ☐
		15	£200	14·00	☐ ☐
		16	£200	14·00	☐ ☐
		17	£225	14·00	☐ ☐
		18	£225	14·00	☐ ☐
		19	£200	14·00	☐ ☐
		20	£200	30·00	☐ ☐
158	3d red	20	£225	35·00	☐ ☐
		21	£180	25·00	☐ ☐
152	4d verm	15	£600	£140	☐ ☐
		16	*	£10000	☐ ☐
153	4d green	15	£450	90·00	☐ ☐
		16	£400	85·00	☐ ☐
		17	*	£6000	☐ ☐
160	4d brown	17	£175	25·00	☐ ☐
		18	£175	25·00	☐ ☐
147	6d grey	13	£225	18·00	☐ ☐
		14	£225	18·00	☐ ☐
		15	£225	16·00	☐ ☐
		16	£225	16·00	☐ ☐
		17	£300	35·00	☐ ☐
161	6d grey	17	£180	20·00	☐ ☐
		18	£150	20·00	☐ ☐
150	1s green	8	£325	32·00	☐ ☐
		9	£325	32·00	☐ ☐
		10	£300	32·00	☐ ☐
		11	£300	32·00	☐ ☐
		12	£250	26·00	☐ ☐
		13	£250	26·00	☐ ☐
		14	*	£10000	☐ ☐
163	1s brown	13	£275	40·00	☐ ☐
		14	£225	40·00	☐ ☐

35

37

38

36

44

45

46

47 Small Anchor

48 Orb

Large coloured corner letters

1873–80 (*i*) *Wmk Small Anchor Type* **47**

139	**41**	2½d mauve *Pl.*	£225	25·00	☐ ☐

(*ii*) *Wmk Orb Type* **48**

| 141 | **41** | 2½d mauve *Pl.* | £200 | 12·00 | ☐ ☐ |
| 142 | | 2½d blue *Pl.* | £175 | 10·00 | ☐ ☐ |

(*iii*) *Wmk Spray of Rose Type* **33**

143	**42**	3d red *Pl.*	£200	12·00	☐ ☐
145	**43**	6d pale buff (Plate 13)	£4500		☐ ☐
147		6d grey *Pl.*	£225	16·00	☐ ☐
150	**44**	1s green *Pl.*	£250	26·00	☐ ☐
151		1s brown (Plate 13)	£1100	£150	☐ ☐

(*iv*) *Wmk Large Garter Type* **17**

152	**45**	4d vermilion *Pl.*	£600	£140	☐ ☐
153		4d green *Pl.*	£400	85·00	☐ ☐
154		4d brown (Plate 17)	£600	£120	☐ ☐
156	**46**	8d orange (Plate 1)	£550	£100	☐ ☐

49 Imperial Crown   **(50)** Surcharges in red **(51)**

1880–83 *Wmk Imperial Crown Type* **49**

157	**41**	2½d blue *Pl.*	£175	8·00	☐ ☐
158	**42**	3d red *Pl.*	£180	25·00	☐ ☐
159		3d on 3d lilac (surch Type **50**)	£225	65·00	☐ ☐
160	**45**	4d brown *Pl.*	£175	25·00	☐ ☐
161	**43**	6d grey *Pl.*	£150	20·00	☐ ☐
162		6d on 6d lilac (surch Type **51**)	£200	60·00	☐ ☐
163	**44**	1s brown *Pl.*	£225	40·00	☐ ☐

---

39 Maltese Cross

40 Large Anchor

1867–83 (*i*) *Wmk Maltese Cross Type* **39**   *Perf* 15½ × 15

126	**35**	5s red *Pl.*	£2500	£250	☐ ☐
128	**36**	10s grey (Plate 1)	£18000	£800	☐ ☐
129	**37**	£1 brown (Plate 1)	£22000	£1100	☐ ☐

(*ii*) *Wmk Large Anchor Type* **40**   *Perf* 14

134	**35**	5s red (Plate 4)	£4500	£800	☐ ☐
131	**36**	10s grey (Plate 1)	£20000	£1000	☐ ☐
132	**37**	£1 brown (Plate 1)	£27000	£2000	☐ ☐
137	**38**	£5 orange (Plate 1)	£4500	£1200	☐ ☐

41

42

43

5

52

53

54

55

56

1880–81 *Wmk Imperial Crown Type* 49

164	**52**	½d green	..	..	15·00	3·00	☐	☐
166	**53**	1d brown	..	..		4·00	2·00	☐	☐
167	**54**	1½d brown	..	..	80·00	14·00	☐	☐
168	**55**	2d red ..	..	..	90·00	30·00	☐	☐
169	**56**	5d indigo	..	..	£350	40·00	☐	☐

57

Die I

Die II

1881 *Wmk Imperial Crown Type* 49
(*a*) 14 *dots in each corner, Die* I

| 171 | **57** | 1d lilac | .. | .. | 75·00 | 12·00 | ☐ | ☐ |

(*b*) 16 *dots in each corner, Die* II

| 174 | **57** | 1d lilac | .. | .. | 80 | 30 | ☐ | ☐ |

58

59

60

Coloured letters in the corners

1883-84 *Wmk Anchor Type* 40

179	**58**	2s 6d deep lilac	..	£200	50·00	☐	☐
181	**59**	5s red ..	..	..	£400	70·00	☐	☐
183	**60**	10s blue ..	..	..	£700	£225	☐	☐

61

1884 *Wmk* 3 *Imperial Crowns Type* 49

| 185 | **61** | £1 brown | .. | ..£10000 | £850 | ☐ | ☐ |

1888 *Wmk* 3 *Orbs Type* 48

| 186 | **61** | £1 brown | .. | ..£16000 | £1200 | ☐ | ☐ |

1891 *Wmk* 3 *Imperial Crowns Type* 49

| 212 | **61** | £1 green | .. | .. £2000 | £350 | ☐ | ☐ |

62

63

64

65

66

1883–84 *Wmk Imperial Crown Type* 49 (*sideways on horiz designs*)

187	**52**	½d blue	..	..	8·00	1·50	☐	☐
188	**62**	1½d lilac	..	..	55·00	18·00	☐	☐
189	**63**	2d lilac	..	..	70·00	25·00	☐	☐
190	**64**	2½d lilac	..	..	40·00	5·00	☐	☐
191	**65**	3d lilac	..	..	90·00	40·00	☐	☐
192	**66**	4d dull green	..	£200	80·00	☐	☐
193	**62**	5d dull green	..	£200'	80·00	☐	☐
194	**63**	6d dull green	..	£225	90·00	☐	☐
195	**64**	9d dull green	..	£475	£200	☐	☐
196	**65**	1s dull green	..	£350	£130	☐	☐

The above prices are for stamps in the true dull green colour. Stamps which have been soaked, causing the colour to run, are virtually worthless.

67

68

69

70

71

72

73

74

75

76

77

78

KING EDWARD VII
1901 (22 Jan.)–1910 (6 May)

79

80

81

82

83

84

85

86

87

88

89

90

91

92

93

'Jubilee' issue
1887–1900 *The bicoloured stamps have the value tablets,*
or the frames including the value tablets, in the second colour.
Wmk Imperial Crown Type **49**

197	**67**	½d	vermilion	..	1·00	50	□ □
213		½d	green*	.. ..	1·00	50	□ □
198	**68**	1½d	purple and green	8·00	3·00		□ □
200	**69**	2d	green and red ..	15·00	5·50		□ □
201	**70**	2½d	purple on blue	10·00	40		□ □
203	**71**	3d	purple on yellow	13·00	1·00		□ □
205a	**72**	4d	green and brown	18·00	6·00		□ □
206	**73**	4½d	purple and red ..	4·50	20·00		□ □
207a	**74**	5d	purple and blue	18·00	5·00		□ □
208	**75**	6d	purple on red ..	18·00	5·00		□ □
209	**76**	9d	purple and blue	40·00	25·00		□ □
210	**77**	10d	purple and red	35·00	22·00		□ □
211	**78**	1s	green	£125	30·00		□ □
214		1s	green and red ..	45·00	70·00		□ □
	Set of 14		.. ..	£300	£180		□ □

* The ½d, No. 213, in blue, has had the colour changed due to exposure to
moisture.

7

1902–13 Wmks Imperial Crown Type **49** (½d to 1s); Anchor Type **40** (2s 6d to 10s); Three Crowns Type **49** (£1)

(a) Perf 14

215	**79**	½d	blue-green ..	1·00	30	□ □
217		½d	yellow-green ..	75	20	□ □
219		1d	red	75	15	□ □
222	**80**	1½d	purple and green	12·00	4·75	□ □
291	**81**	2d	green and red ..	10·00	4·50	□ □
231	**82**	2½d	blue	4·50	2·50	□ □
234	**83**	3d	purple on yellow	13·00	6·00	□ □
237	**84**	4d	green and brown	22·00	7·00	□ □
240		4d	orange ..	11·00	6·50	□ □
294	**85**	5d	purple and blue	11·00	4·75	□ □
245	**79**	6d	purple	15·00	4·00	□ □
249	**86**	7d	grey	4·25	6·00	□ □
307	**87**	9d	purple and blue	40·00	22·00	□ □
311	**88**	10d	purple and red ..	35·00	20·00	□ □
314	**89**	1s	green and red ..	28·00	8·00	□ □
316	**90**	2s 6d	lilac	£135	45·00	□ □
263	**91**	5s	red	£200	55·00	□ □
265	**92**	10s	blue	£475	£200	□ □
320	**93**	£1	green	£1100	£275	□ □
		Set of 15 (to 1s)		£190	85·00	□ □

(b) Perf 15×14

279	**79**	½d	green	20·00	25·00	□ □
281		1d	red	5·00	3·00	□ □
283	**82**	2½d	blue	11·00	5·00	□ □
285	**83**	3d	purple on yellow	18·00	3·50	□ □
286	**84**	4d	orange	13·00	6·00	□ □
		Set of 5		60·00	35·00	□ □

KING GEORGE V
1910 (6 May)–1936 (20 Jan.)

PERFORATION. All the following issues are Perf 15×14 except vertical commemorative stamps which are 14×15, unless otherwise stated.

94 (Hair dark)   95 (Lion unshaded)   96

1911–12 Wmk Imperial Crown Type **49**

322	**94**	½d	green	2·25	75	□ □
327	**95**	1d	red	2·00	90	□ □

1912 Wmk Royal Cypher ('Simple') Type **96**

335	**94**	½d	green	28·00	22·00	□ □
336	**95**	1d	red	15·00	12·00	□ □

97 (Hair light)   98 (Lion shaded)   99

1912 Wmk Imperial Crown Type **49**

340	**97**	½d	green	2·50	75	□ □
342	**98**	1d	red	1·00	50	□ □

1912 Wmk Royal Cypher ('Simple') Type **96**

344	**97**	½d	green	3·00	60	□ □
345	**98**	1d	red	2·50	50	□ □

1912 Wmk Royal Cypher ('Multiple') Type **99**

348	**97**	½d	green	5·00	2·50	□ □
349	**98**	1d	red	6·50	4·00	□ □

100   101   102

103   104

1912–24 Wmk Royal Cypher Type **96**

351	**101**	½d	green	40	15	□ □
357	**100**	1d	red	25	15	□ □
362	**101**	1½d	brown	80	15	□ □
368	**102**	2d	orange	90	35	□ □
372	**100**	2½d	blue	4·00	1·00	□ □
375	**102**	3d	violet	2·00	75	□ □
379		4d	grey-green ..	4·50	75	□ □
382	**103**	5d	brown	4·50	2·25	□ □
385		6d	purple	7·00	1·00	□ □
			a. Perf 14	60·00	80·00	□ □
387		7d	olive-green ..	9·00	3·75	□ □
390		8d	black on yellow	20·00	6·50	□ □
392	**104**	9d	black	7·00	2·00	□ □
393a		9d	olive-green ..	65·00	14·00	□ □
394		10d	blue	13·00	11·00	□ □
395		1s	brown	7·50	1·00	□ □
		Set of 15		£130	38·00	□ □

1913 *Wmk Royal Cypher ('Multiple')* Type **99**

397	**101**	½d green	..	..	75·00	90·00	□ □
398	**100**	1d red ..	..	..	£150	£130	□ □

See also Nos. 418/29.

105

106

T 105. Background around portrait consists of horizontal lines

1913–18 *Wmk Single Cypher Type* **106** *Perf* 11 × 12

413a	**105**	2s 6d brown	..	..	70·00	25·00	□ □
416		5s red ..	..	..	£175	35·00	□ □
417		10s blue	..	..	£300	80·00	□ □
403		£1 green	..	..	£1250	£600	□ □
	Set of 4	..	..	..	£1600	£700	□ □

See also Nos. 450/2.

107

1924–26 *Wmk Block Cypher Type* **107**

418	**101**	½d green	..	..	15	15	□ □
419	**100**	1d red ..	..	..	25	25	□ □
420	**101**	1½d brown	..	..	20	20	□ □
421	**102**	2d orange	..	..	1·00	60	□ □
422	**100**	2½d blue	..	..	4·50	90	□ □
423	**102**	3d violet	..	..	5·50	60	□ □
424		4d grey-green	..	..	7·50	90	□ □
425	**103**	5d brown	..	..	17·00	1·40	□ □
426a		6d purple	..	..	2·00	35	□ □
427	**104**	9d olive-green	..	..	9·00	2·25	□ □
428		10d blue	..	..	24·00	16·00	□ □
429		1s brown	..	..	16·00	75	□ □
	Set of 12	..	..	..	75·00	20·00	□ □

For full information on all future British issues, collectors should write to the British Post Office Philatelic Bureau, 20 Brandon Street, Edinburgh EH3 5TT

108

109

British Empire Exhibition

1924–25 *Wmk* **107** *Perf* 14

(*a*) 23.4.24. *Dated* '1924'

430	**108**	1d red ..	..	..	4·00	6·00	□ □
431	**109**	1½d brown	..	..	6·50	11·00	□ □
	First Day Cover	..	..	..		£350	□

(*b*) 9.5.25. *Dated* '1925'

432	**108**	1d red ..	..	..	9·00	17·00	□ □
433	**109**	1½d brown	..	..	25·00	50·00	□ □
	First Day Cover	..	..	..		£1200	□

110

111

112

113 St George and the Dragon

114

9

Ninth Universal Postal Union Congress

1929 (10 MAY) (a) *Wmk* **107**

434	**110**	½d green	..	..	1·00	90	□ □
435	**111**	1d red ..	..	..	1·00	1·00	□ □
436		1½d brown		..	1·00	90	□ □
437	**112**	2½d blue		..	5·00	9·00	□ □

(b) *Wmk* **114** *Perf* 12

438	**113**	£1 black	..	..	£650	£450	□ □
434/7	*Set of 4*		..	..	7·00	11·00	□ □
434/7	*First Day Cover (4 vals.)*					£500	□
434/8	*First Day Cover (5 vals.)*			..		£2500	□

115

116

117

118

119

1934–36 *Wmk* **107**

439	**115**	½d green	..	..	15	15	□ □
440	**116**	1d red ..	..	..	15	15	□ □
441	**115**	1½d brown	..	..	10	15	□ □
442	**117**	2d orange	..	..	30	30	□ □
443	**116**	2½d blue	..	..	1·25	60	□ □
444	**117**	3d violet	..	..	1·00	50	□ □
445		4d grey-green		..	1·50	55	□ □
446	**118**	5d brown	..	..	5·00	1·50	□ □
447	**119**	9d olive-green	..	..	9·00	1·60	□ □
448		10d blue	..	..	14·00	8·00	□ □
449		1s brown	..	..	12·00	50	□ □
	Set of 11		..	..	35·00	11·00	□ □

T 105 (re-engraved). *Background around portrait consists of horizontal and diagonal lines*

1934 *Wmk* **106** *Perf* 11 × 12

450	**105**	2s 6d brown	..	..	50·00	15·00	□ □
451		5s red ..	..	..	£100	30·00	□ □
452		10s blue	..	..	£200	40·00	□ □
	Set of 3		..	..	£300	75·00	□ □

120

121

122   123

Silver Jubilee

1935 (7 MAY) *Wmk* **107**

453	**120**	½d green	..	..	50	20	□ □
454	**121**	1d red ..	..	..	75	90	□ □
455	**122**	1½d brown	..	..	50	20	□ □
456	**123**	2½d blue	..	..	3·00	5·50	□ □
	Set of 4		..	..	4·25	6·00	□ □
	First Day Cover		..	..		£400	□

KING EDWARD VIII
1936 (20 Jan.–10 Dec.)

124   125

1936 *Wmk* **125**

457	**124**	½d green	..	..	20	15	□ □
458		1d red ..	..	..	50	20	□ □
459		1½d brown	..	..	25	15	□ □
460		2½d blue	..	..	25	60	□ □
	Set of 4		..	..	1·00	1·00	□ □

KING GEORGE VI
1936 (11 Dec.)–1952 (6 Feb.)

126 King George VI
and Queen Elizabeth

127

131 King George VI

131a

132

132a

Coronation

1937 (13 MAY) *Wmk* **127**

461	**126**	1½d brown	..	..	40	25	□	□
		First Day Cover	..	..		28·00		□

128   **129**   **130**

King George VI and National Emblems

133

1939–48 *Wmk* **133**   *Perf* 14

476	**131**	2s 6d brown	..	..	45·00	9·00	□	□
476a		2s 6d green	..	..	15·00	90	□	□
477	**131a**	5s red	..	..	20·00	1·25	□	□
478	**132**	10s dark blue	..	£160	18·00		□	□
478a		10s bright blue	..	50·00	4·00		□	□
478b	**132a**	£1 brown	..	..	25·00	22·00	□	□
		Set of 6	..	..	£275	48·00	□	□

1937–47 *Wmk* **127**

462	**128**	½d green	..	..	10	15	□	□
463		1d scarlet	..	..	10	15	□	□
464		1½d brown	..	..	20	15	□	□
465		2d orange	..	..	1·25	35	□	□
466		2½d blue	..	..	25	15	□	□
467		3d violet	..	..	6·00	60	□	□
468	**129**	4d green	..	..	35	30	□	□
469		5d brown	..	..	2·50	35	□	□
470		6d purple	..	..	1·75	25	□	□
471	**130**	7d green	..	..	4·50	35	□	□
472		8d red	..	..	5·00	40	□	□
473		9d deep green	..	..	6·50	40	□	□
474		10d blue	..	..	5·00	45	□	□
474a		11d plum	..	..	3·00	1·25	□	□
475		1s brown	..	..	5·00	25	□	□
		Set of 15	..	..	38·00	5·00	□	□

For later printings of the lower values in apparently lighter shades and different colours, see Nos. 485/90 and 503/8.

For full information on all future British issues, collectors should write to the British Post Office Philatelic Bureau, 20 Brandon Street, Edinburgh EH3 5TT

134 Queen Victoria and King George VI

Centenary of First Adhesive Postage Stamps

1940 (6 MAY) *Wmk* **127**   *Perf* 14½ × 14

479	**134**	½d green	..	..	30	20	□	□
480		1d red	..	..	90	40	□	□
481		1½d brown	..	..	30	30	□	□
482		2d orange	..	..	50	40	□	□
483		2½d blue	..	..	1·90	80	□	□
484		3d violet	..	..	4·00	4·00	□	□
		Set of 6	..	..	7·00	5·50	□	□
		First Day Cover	..	..		28·00		□

Head as Nos. 462/7, but lighter background

1941–42 *Wmk* **127**

485	**128**	½d pale green	..	15	10	☐	☐
486		1d pale red	.. ..	15	10	☐	☐
487		1½d pale brown	..	65	35	☐	☐
488		2d pale orange	..	50	25	☐	☐
489		2½d light blue	..	15	10	☐	☐
490		3d pale violet	..	1·60	30	☐	☐
	Set of 6	.. .. ..		2·75	1·10	☐	☐

135 Symbols of Peace and Reconstruction

136 Symbols of Peace and Reconstruction

Victory

1946 (11 JUNE) *Wmk* **127**

491	**135**	2½d blue	.. ..	20	15	☐	☐
492	**136**	3d violet	.. ..	20	10	☐	☐
	First Day Cover	.. .. ..		45·00			☐

137 King George VI and Queen Elizabeth

138 King George VI and Queen Elizabeth

Royal Silver Wedding

1948 (26 APR.) *Wmk* **127**

493	**137**	2½d blue	..	20	20	☐	☐
494	**138**	£1 blue	..	40·00	35·00	☐	☐
	First Day Cover	.. ..		£350			☐

1948 (10 MAY)

Stamps of 1d and 2½d showing seaweed-gathering were on sale at eight Head Post Offices elsewhere in Great Britain, but were primarily for use in the Channel Islands and are listed there (see after Regional Issues).

139 Globe and Laurel Wreath

140 'Speed'

141 Olympic Symbol

142 Winged Victory

Olympic Games

1948 (29 JULY) *Wmk* **127**

495	**139**	2½d blue	.. ..	10	10	☐	☐
496	**140**	3d violet	.. ..	30	20	☐	☐
497	**141**	6d purple	.. ..	50	20	☐	☐
498	**142**	1s brown	.. ..	1·60	1·25	☐	☐
	Set of 4	.. ..		2·25	1·50	☐	☐
	First Day Cover	.. ..			30·00		☐

143 Two Hemispheres

144 U.P.U. Monument, Berne

145 Goddess Concordia, Globe and Points of Compass

146 Posthorn and Globe

75th Anniversary of Universal Postal Union

1949 (10 OCT.) *Wmk* **127**

499	**143**	2½d blue	.. ..	10	10	☐	☐
500	**144**	3d violet	.. ..	30	30	☐	☐
501	**145**	6d purple	.. ..	55	55	☐	☐
502	**146**	1s brown	.. ..	1·60	1·40	☐	☐
	Set of 4	.. .. ..		2·25	2·00	☐	☐
	First Day Cover				55·00		☐

4d as No. 468 and others as Nos. 485/9, but colours changed

1950–52 *Wmk* 127

503	**128**	½d pale orange ..		10	15	☐	☐
504		1d light blue		10	15	☐	☐
505		1½d pale green		25	30	☐	☐
506		2d pale brown		25	20	☐	☐
507		2½d pale red ..		20	15	☐	☐
508	**129**	4d light blue		1·40	1·10	☐	☐
	Set of 6	.. .. ..		2·00	1·75	☐	☐

147 HMS *Victory*

148 White Cliffs of Dover

149 St George and the Dragon

150 Royal Coat of Arms

1951 (3 MAY) *Wmk* **133** *Perf* 11 × 12

509	**147**	2s 6d green	.. ..	10·00	75	☐	☐
510	**148**	5s red ..	.. ..	28·00	1·50	☐	☐
511	**149**	10s blue	.. ..	20·00	6·00	☐	☐
512	**150**	£1 brown	.. ..	32·00	16·00	☐	☐
	Set of 4	.. ..	.. ..	80·00	20·00	☐	☐

151 Commerce and Prosperity

152 Festival Symbol

Festival of Britain

1951 (3 MAY) *Wmk* 127

513	**151**	2½d red ..	.. ..	20	10	☐	☐
514	**152**	4d blue	.. ..	40	35	☐	☐
	First Day Cover	.. .. ..		16·00		☐	

QUEEN ELIZABETH II
6 February, 1952

153 Tudor Crown

154

155

156

157

158

159

160

Queen Elizabeth II and National Emblems

1952–54 *Wmk* **153**

515	**154**	½d orange	.. ..	10	15	☐	☐
516		1d blue	.. ..	20	20	☐	☐
517		1½d green	.. ..	10	15	☐	☐
518		2d brown	.. ..	20	15	☐	☐
519	**155**	2½d red ..	.. ..	10	15	☐	☐
520		3d lilac	.. ..	1·00	30	☐	☐
521	**156**	4d blue	.. ..	3·00	80	☐	☐
		4½d (*See Nos.* 577, 594, 609 *and* 616b)					
522	**157**	5d brown	.. ..	90	2·00	☐	☐
523		6d purple	.. ..	2·50	60	☐	☐
524		7d green	.. ..	10·00	3·50	☐	☐
525	**158**	8d magenta ..	..	90	60	☐	☐
526		9d bronze-green	..	22·00	3·00	☐	☐
527		10d blue	.. ..	18·00	3·00	☐	☐
528		11d plum	.. ..	30·00	16·00	☐	☐
529	**159**	1s bistre	.. ..	90	40	☐	☐
530	**160**	1s 3d green	.. ..	5·00	2·00	☐	☐
531	**159**	1s 6d indigo	.. ..	12·00	2·25	☐	☐
	Set of 17	.. ..		95·00	28·00	☐	☐

See also Nos. 540/56, 561/6, 570/94 and 599/618a.
For First Day Cover prices see page 36.

161

162

163

164

Coronation

1953 (3 JUNE) *Wmk* **153**

532	**161**	2½d red ..	..	..	10	10	☐	☐
533	**162**	4d blue	..	..	30	70	☐	☐
534	**163**	1s 3d green	..	..	5·00	4·00	☐	☐
535	**164**	1s 6d blue	..	..	8·00	7·00	☐	☐
		Set of 4	..	..	12·00	10·00	☐	☐
		First Day Cover	..	..		32·00		☐

165 St Edward's Crown

166 Carrickfergus Castle

167 Caernarvon Castle

168 Edinburgh Castle

169 Windsor Castle

1955–58 *Wmk* **165** *Perf* 11 × 12

536	**166**	2s 6d brown	..	..	8·00	1·50	☐	☐
537	**167**	5s red ..	..	..	40·00	3·00	☐	☐
538	**168**	10s blue	..	..	£100	10·00	☐	☐
539	**169**	£1 black	..	..	£160	25·00	☐	☐
		Set of 4	..	..	£275	35·00	☐	☐

See also Nos. 595a/8a, 759/62 and F.D.C's on page 36.

1955–58 *Wmk* **165**

540	**154**	½d orange	..	..	10	15	☐	☐
541		1d blue	..	..	25	15	☐	☐
542		1½d green	..	..	10	15	☐	☐
543		2d red-brown	..	..	20	20	☐	☐
543b		2d light red-brown			20	15	☐	☐
544	**155**	2½d red ..	..	..	15	15	☐	☐
545		3d lilac	..	..	20	15	☐	☐
546	**156**	4d blue	..	..	1·25	40	☐	☐
547	**157**	5d brown	..	..	5·50	2·75	☐	☐
548a		6d purple	..	..	2·50	80	☐	☐
549		7d green	..	..	38·00	7·50	☐	☐
550	**158**	8d magenta	..	..	6·50	1·00	☐	☐
551		9d bronze-green	..		12·00	1·50	☐	☐
552		10d blue	..	..	12·00	1·50	☐	☐
553		11d plum	..	..	40	1·00	☐	☐
554	**159**	1s bistre	..	..	11·00	40	☐	☐
555	**160**	1s 3d green	..	..	15·00	1·25	☐	☐
556	**159**	1s 6d indigo	..	..	20·00	1·00	☐	☐
		Set of 18	..	..	£110	18·00	☐	☐

170 Scout Badge and 'Rolling Hitch'

171 'Scouts coming to Britain'

172 Globe within a Compass

173

World Scout Jubilee Jamboree

1957 (1 AUG.) *Wmk* **165**

557	**170**	2½d red ..	..	..	15	10	☐	☐
558	**171**	4d blue	..	..	50	40	☐	☐
559	**172**	1s 3d green	..	..	6·00	5·00	☐	☐
		Set of 3	..	..	6·00	5·00	☐	☐
		First Day Cover	..	..		12·00		☐

46th Inter Parliamentary Union Conference

1957 (12 SEPT.) *Wmk* **165**

560	**173**	4d blue	..	..	1·10	1·10	☐	☐
		First Day Cover	..	..		80·00		☐

Graphite-lined and Phosphor Issues

These are used in connection with automatic sorting machinery, originally experimentally at Southampton but now also operating elsewhere. In such areas these stamps were the normal issue, but from mid 1967 *all* low-value stamps bear phosphor markings.

The graphite lines were printed in black on the back, beneath the gum; two lines per stamp except for the 2d (*see below*).

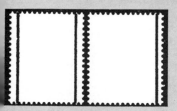

174   **175** (2d only)
(Stamps viewed from back)

In November 1959, phosphor bands, printed on the front, replaced the graphite. They are wider than the graphite, not easy to see, but show as broad vertical bands at certain angles to the light.

Values representing the rate for printed papers (and second class mail from 1968) have one band and others have two, three or four bands according to size and format. From 1972 onwards some commemorative stamps were printed with 'all-over' phosphor.

In the small stamps the bands are on each side with the single band at left (except where otherwise stated). In the large-size commemorative stamps the single band may be at left, centre or right varying in different issues. The bands are vertical on both horizontal and vertical designs except where otherwise stated.

See also notes on page 35.

Graphite-lined issue

1957 (19 Nov.) *Two graphite lines on the back, except 2d value, which has one line. Wmk* **165**

561	**154**	½d	orange	..	..	20	30	☐	☐
562		1d	blue	..	..	20	35	☐	☐
563		1½d	green	..	..	40	1·25	☐	☐
564		2d	light red-brown		..	3·00	1·50	☐	☐
565	**155**	2½d	red	..	..	7·00	8·00	☐	☐
566		3d	lilac	..	..	50	50	☐	☐
	Set of 6		..	..	..	10·00	11·00	☐	☐

See also Nos. 587/94.

For First Day Cover price see page 36.

176 Welsh Dragon   **177** Flag and Games Emblem

178 Welsh Dragon

Sixth British Empire and Commonwealth Games, Cardiff

1958 (18 JULY) *Wmk* **165**

567	**176**	3d	lilac	..	..	15	10	☐	☐
568	**177**	6d	mauve	..	..	25	20	☐	☐
569	**178**	1s 3d	green	..	..	2·75	2·00	☐	☐
	Set of 3		..	..	..	2·75	2·10	☐	☐
	First Day Cover		..	..	..		50·00		☐

179 Multiple Crowns

WATERMARK. All the following issues to No. 755 are Watermark **179** (sideways on the vertical commemorative stamps) unless otherwise stated.

1958–65 *Wmk* **179**

570	**154**	½d	orange	..	..	10	10	☐	☐
571		1d	blue	..	..	10	10	☐	☐
572		1½d	green	..	..	10	15	☐	☐
573		2d	light red-brown		..	10	10	☐	☐
574	**155**	2½d	red	..	..	10	10	☐	☐
575		3d	lilac	..	..	10	10	☐	☐
576a	**156**	4d	blue	..	..	15	10	☐	☐
577		4½d	brown	..	..	10	15	☐	☐
578	**157**	5d	brown	..	..	20	20	☐	☐
579		6d	purple	..	..	15	15	☐	☐
580		7d	green	..	..	30	20	☐	☐
581	**158**	8d	magenta	..	..	45	15	☐	☐
582		9d	bronze-green	..	..	35	15	☐	☐
583		10d	blue	..	..	90	15	☐	☐
584	**159**	1s	bistre	..	..	30	15	☐	☐
585	**160**	1s 3d	green	..	..	25	15	☐	☐
586	**159**	1s 6d	indigo	..	..	4·00	40	☐	☐
	Set of 17		..	..	..	6·00	2·10	☐	☐

For 4½d on First Day Cover see page 36.

For full information on all future British issues, collectors should write to the British Post Office Philatelic Bureau, 20 Brandon Street, Edinburgh EH3 5TT

Graphite-lined issue

1958–61 *Two graphite lines on the back, except 2d value, which has one line. Wmk* **179**

587	154	½d orange	.. ..	4·00	3·00	☐	☐
588		1d blue	.. ..	90	1·25	☐	☐
589		1½d green	.. ..	30·00	30·00	☐	☐
590		2d light red-brown		7·00	4·00	☐	☐
591	155	2½d red ..	.. ..	10·00	10·00	☐	☐
592		3d lilac	.. ..	40	40	☐	☐
593	156	4d blue	.. ..	4·00	4·50	☐	☐
594		4½d brown	.. ..	4·00	4·00	☐	☐
		Set of 8	.. ..	55·00	45·00	☐	☐

The prices quoted for No. 589 are for examples with inverted watermark. Stamps with upright watermark are *priced at £85 mint*, £60 *used*.

1959–63 *Wmk* **179**   *Perf* 11 × 12

595a	166	2s 6d brown	.. ..	40	30	☐	☐
596a	167	5s red ..	.. ..	1·00	60	☐	☐
597a	168	10s blue	.. ..	2·25	3·00	☐	☐
598a	169	£1 black	.. ..	9·50	5·00	☐	☐
		Set of 4	.. ..	12·00	8·00	☐	☐

Phosphor-Graphite issue

1959 (18 Nov.) *Two phosphor bands on front and two graphite lines on back, except 2d value, which has one band on front and one line on back*

(a) Wmk **165**

599	154	½d orange	.. ..	3·50	5·00	☐	☐
600		1d blue	.. ..	3·50	4·50	☐	☐
601		1½d green	.. ..	3·50	4·50	☐	☐

(b) Wmk **179**

605	154	2d light red-brown (1 band)	.. ..	5·00	4·50	☐	☐
606	155	2½d red ..	.. ..	15·00	11·00	☐	☐
607		3d lilac	.. ..	11·00	7·50	☐	☐
608	156	4d blue	.. ..	12·00	27·00	☐	☐
609		4½d brown	.. ..	30·00	18·00	☐	☐
		Set of 8	, ...	75·00	75·00	☐	☐

Phosphor issue

1960–67 *Two phosphor bands on front, except where otherwise stated. Wmk* **179**

610	154	½d orange	.. ..	10	15	☐	☐
611		1d blue	.. ..	10	10	☐	☐
612		1½d green	.. ..	10	20	☐	☐
613		2d light red-brown (1 band) ..		22·00	20·00	☐	☐
613a		2d light red-brown (2 bands)		10	10	☐	☐
614	155	2½d red (2 bands) ..		10	40	☐	☐
614a		2½d red (1 band) ..		40	75	☐	☐
615		3d lilac (2 bands)		60	45	☐	☐
615c		3d lilac (1 side band)	..	35	60	☐	☐
615e		3d lilac (1 centre band)	.. ..	25	40	☐	☐

616a	156	4d blue	.. ..	15	15	☐	☐
616b		4½d brown	.. ..	15	25	☐	☐
616c	157	5d brown	.. ..	20	25	☐	☐
617		6d purple	.. ..	40	20	☐	☐
617a		7d green	.. ..	60	25	☐	☐
617b	158	8d magenta ..	.. ..	20	25	☐	☐
617c		9d bronze-green	..	60	25	☐	☐
617d		10d blue	.. ..	80	35	☐	☐
617e	159	1s bistre	.. ..	40	20	☐	☐
618	160	1s 3d green	.. ..	2·00	2·50	☐	☐
618a	159	1s 6d indigo	.. ..	1·60	1·00	☐	☐
		Set of 17 (one of each value)		7·00	6·00	☐	☐

No. 615c exists with the phosphor band at the left or right of the stamp.

180 Postboy of 1660   181 Posthorn of 1660

Tercentenary of Establishment of 'General Letter Office'

1960 (7 July)

619	180	3d lilac	.. ..	20	10	☐	☐
620	181	1s 3d green	.. ..	4·50	4·25	☐	☐
		Set of 2	.. ..	4·50	4·25	☐	☐
		First Day Cover ..	.. ..		38·00		☐

182 Conference Emblem

First Anniversary of European Postal and Telecommunications Conference

1960 (19 Sept.)

621	182	6d green and purple		40	60	☐	☐
622		1s 6d brown and blue		6·50	5·50	☐	☐
		Set of 2	.. .. ..	6·50	5·50	☐	☐
		First Day Cover ..	.. ..		27·00		☐

183 Thrift Plant   184 'Growth of Savings'

185 Thrift Plant

Centenary of Post Office Savings Bank

1961 (28 Aug.)

623	**183**	2½d black and red ..	10	10	□	□
624	**184**	3d orange-brown and violet ..	10	10	□	□
625	**185**	1s 6d red and blue ..	2·60	2·00	□	□
	Set of 3		2·60	2·00	□	□
	First Day Cover			55·00		□

186 C.E.P.T. Emblem

187 Doves and Emblem

188 Doves and Emblem

European Postal and Telecommunications (C.E.P.T.) Conference, Torquay

1961 (18 Sept.)

626	**186**	2d orange, pink and brown	10	10	□	□
627	**187**	4d buff, mauve and ultramarine ..	20	10	□	□
628	**188**	10d turquoise, green and blue	40	25	□	□
	Set of 3		60	40	□	□
	First Day Cover			2·50		□

189 Hammer Beam Roof, Westminster Hall

190 Palace of Westminster

Seventh Commonwealth Parliamentary Conference

1961 (25 Sept.)

629	**189**	6d purple and gold	25	20	□	□
630	**190**	1s 3d green and blue	2·75	2·00	□	□
	Set of 2		3·00	2·10	□	□
	First Day Cover			24·00		□

191 'Units of Productivity'

192 'National Productivity'

193 'Unified Productivity'

National Productivity Year

1962 (14 Nov.) *Wmk* **179** (*inverted on* 2½d *and* 3d)

631	**191**	2½d green and red ..	20	10	□	□
		p. Phosphor ..	1·00	40	□	□
632	**192**	3d blue and violet	25	10	□	□
		p. Phosphor ..	1·00	50	□	□
633	**193**	1s 3d red, blue and green	2·50	1·60	□	□
		p. Phosphor ..	28·00	21·00	□	□
	Set of 3 (Ordinary)		2·75	1·60	□	□
	Set of 3 (Phosphor)		28·00	21·00	□	□
	First Day Cover (Ordinary) ..			24·00		□
	First Day Cover (Phosphor)			70·00		□

194 Campaign Emblem and Family

195 Children of Three Races

Freedom from Hunger

1963 (21 Mar.) *Wmk* **179** (*inverted*)

634	**194**	2½d crimson and pink	10	10	□	□
		p. Phosphor ..	1·00	1·00	□	□
635	**195**	1s 3d brown and yellow	2·75	2·50	□	□
		p. Phosphor ..	26·00	22·00	□	□
	Set of 2 (Ordinary)		2·75	2·50	□	□
	Set of 2 (Phosphor)		27·00	23·00	□	□
	First Day Cover (Ordinary) ..			24·00		□
	First Day Cover (Phosphor)..			25·00		□

196 'Paris Conference'

Paris Postal Conference Centenary
1963 (7 MAY) *Wmk 179 (inverted)*

636	**196**	6d green and mauve	60	40	☐	☐
		p. Phosphor	7·50	6·50	☐	☐
		First Day Cover (Ordinary) ..		12·00		☐
		First Day Cover (Phosphor) ..		22·00		☐

197 Posy of Flowers

198 Woodland Life

National Nature Week
1963 (16 MAY)

637	**197**	3d multicoloured ..	20	20	☐	☐
		p. Phosphor ..	50	50	☐	☐
638	**198**	4½d multicoloured ..	40	40	☐	☐
		p. Phosphor ..	3·50	3·00	☐	☐
		Set of 2 (Ordinary)	60	60	☐	☐
		Set of 2 (Phosphor)	4·00	3·50	☐	☐
		First Day Cover (Ordinary) ..		12·00		☐
		First Day Cover (Phosphor)		24·00		☐

199 Rescue at Sea   200 19th·century Lifeboat

201 Lifeboatmen

Ninth International Lifeboat Conference, Edinburgh
1963 (31 MAY)

639	**199**	2½d blue, black and				
		red	10	10	☐	☐
		p. Phosphor ..	40	50	☐	☐
640	**200**	4d multicoloured ..	40	30	☐	☐
		p. Phosphor ..	20	50	☐	☐
641	**201**	1s 6d sepia, yellow				
		and blue ..	4·50	4·00		☐
		p. Phosphor ..	32·00	28·00		☐
		Set of 3 (Ordinary)	4·50	4·00	☐	☐
		Set of 3 (Phosphor)	32·00	28·00	☐	☐
		First Day Cover (Ordinary) ..		25·00		☐
		First Day Cover (Phosphor) ..		30·00		☐

202 Red Cross   203

204   205 'Commonwealth Cable'

Red Cross Centenary Congress
1963 (15 AUG.)

642	**202**	3d red and lilac ..	10	10	☐	☐
		p. Phosphor ..	60	60	☐	☐
643	**203**	1s 3d red, blue and				
		grey	3·25	2·75		☐
		p. Phosphor ..	45·00	35·00	☐	☐
644	**204**	1s 6d red, blue and				
		bistre ..	3·25	2·75		☐
		p. Phosphor ..	30·00	20·00	☐	☐
		Set of 3 (Ordinary)	6·00	5·00	☐	☐
		Set of 3 (Phosphor)	70·00	50·00	☐	☐
		First Day Cover (Ordinary) ..		25·00		☐
		First Day Cover (Phosphor)		60·00		☐

Opening of COMPAC (Trans-Pacific Telephone Cable)
1963 (3 DEC.)

645	**205**	1s 6d blue and black ..	4·00	3·25	☐	☐
		p. Phosphor ..	20·00	20·00	☐	☐
		First Day Cover (Ordinary) ..		20·00		☐
		First Day Cover (Phosphor) ..		24·00		☐

206 Puck and Bottom (*A Midsummer Night's Dream*)

207 Feste (*Twelfth Night*)

208 Balcony Scene (*Romeo and Juliet*)

209 'Eve of Agincourt' (*Henry V*)

210 Hamlet contemplating Yorick's skull (*Hamlet*) and Queen Elizabeth II

Shakespeare Festival

1964 (23 Apr.)   Perf 11 × 12 (2s 6d) *or* 15 × 14 (*others*).

646	**206**	3d bis, blk & vio-bl	10	10	☐	☐
		p. Phosphor ..	20	20	☐	☐
647	**207**	6d multicoloured ..	20	20	☐	☐
		p. Phosphor ..	60	40	☐	☐
648	**208**	1s 3d multicoloured ..	1·00	1·25	☐	☐
		p. Phosphor ..	7·00	6·50	☐	☐
649	**209**	1s 6d multicoloured ..	1·25	1·25	☐	☐
		p. Phosphor ..	12·00	6·50	☐	☐
650	**210**	2s 6d deep slate-purple	2·00	2·00	☐	☐
		Set of 5 (Ordinary) ..	4·25	4·25	☐	☐
		Set of 4 (Phosphor) ..	18·00	12·50	☐	☐
		First Day Cover (Ordinary)		10·00		☐
		First Day Cover (Phosphor)		12·50		☐
		Presentation Pack (Ordinary)	7·50		☐	

PRESENTATION PACKS were first introduced by the G.P.O. for the Shakespeare Festival issue. The packs include one set of stamps and details of the designs, the designer and the stamp printer. They were issued for almost all later definitive and special issues.

For note about Presentation Packs in foreign languages, see page 25.

211 Flats near Richmond Park ('Urban Development')

212 Shipbuilding Yards, Belfast ('Industrial Activity')

213 Beddgelert Forest Park, Snowdonia ('Forestry')

214 Nuclear Reactor, Dounreay ('Technological Development')

20th International Geographical Congress, London

1964 (1 July)

651	**211**	2½d multicoloured ..	10	10	☐	☐
		p. Phosphor	50	40	☐	☐
652	**212**	4d multicoloured ..	25	25	☐	☐
		p. Phosphor	90	70	☐	☐
653	**213**	8d multicoloured ..	50	50	☐	☐
		p. Phosphor	2·00	1·75	☐	☐
654	**214**	1s 6d multicoloured ..	4·00	3·75	☐	☐
		p. Phosphor	28·00	25·00	☐	☐
		Set of 4 (Ordinary) ..	4·50	4·25	☐	☐
		Set of 4 (Phosphor) ..	28·00	25·00	☐	☐
		First Day Cover (Ordinary) ..		18·00		☐
		First Day Cover (Phosphor)		25·00		☐
		Presentation Pack (Ordinary)	85·00		☐	

215 Spring Gentian

216 Dog Rose

217 Honeysuckle

218 Fringed Water Lily

Tenth International Botanical Congress, Edinburgh

1964 (5 Aug.)

655	**215**	3d vio, blue & green	10	10	☐	☐
		p. Phosphor ..	20	20	☐	☐
656	**216**	6d multicoloured ..	20	20	☐	☐
		p. Phosphor ..	1·25	1·40	☐	☐
657	**217**	9d multicoloured ..	2·25	2·25	☐	☐
		p. Phosphor ..	3·75	5·00	☐	☐
658	**218**	1s 3d multicoloured ..	3·00	2·10	☐	☐
		p. Phosphor ..	26·00	26·00	☐	☐
		Set of 4 (Ordinary) ..	5·00	4·25	☐	☐
		Set of 4 (Phosphor) ..	28·00	28·00	☐	☐
		First Day Cover (Ordinary) ..		18·00		☐
		First Day Cover (Phosphor)		28·00		☐
		Presentation Pack (Ordinary)	85·00		☐	

219 Forth Road Bridge

220 Forth Road and
Railway Bridges

Opening of Forth Road Bridge

1964 (4 SEPT.)

659	**219**	3d black, blue and violet	15	10	□	□
		p. Phosphor	50	50	□	□
660	**220**	6d black, blue and red	45	40	□	□
		p. Phosphor	5·00	5·50	□	□
	Set of 2 (Ordinary)		60	50	□	□
	Set of 2 (Phosphor)		5·50	6·00	□	□
	First Day Cover (Ordinary)		5·00		□	
	First Day Cover (Phosphor)		7·00		□	
	Presentation Pack (Ordinary)	£180			□	

221 Sir Winston Churchill

222 Sir Winston Churchill

Churchill Commemoration

1965 (8 JULY)

661	**221**	4d black and drab	15	10	□	□
		p. Phosphor	30	30	□	□
662	**222**	1s 3d black and grey	45	30	□	□
		p. Phosphor	4·00	3·50	□	□
	Set of 2 (Ordinary)		60	40	□	□
	Set of 2 (Phosphor)		4·25	3·75	□	□
	First Day Cover (Ordinary)		2·00		□	
	First Day Cover (Phosphor)		4·50		□	
	Presentation Pack (Ordinary)	10·00			□	

223 Simon de Montfort's Seal

224 Parliament Buildings
(after engraving by Hollar, 1647)

700th Anniversary of Simon de Montfort's Parliament

1965 (19 JULY)

663	**223**	6d green	10	10	□	□
		p. Phosphor	40	40	□	□
664	**224**	2s 6d black, grey and drab	1·25	1·25	□	□
	Set of 2 (Ordinary)		1·25	1·25	□	□
	First Day Cover (Ordinary)		10·00		□	
	First Day Cover (Phosphor)		9·00		□	
	Presentation Pack (Ordinary)	32·00			□	

225 Bandsmen and Banner

226 Three Salvationists

Salvation Army Centenary

1965 (9 AUG.)

665	**225**	3d multicoloured	10	10	□	□
		p. Phosphor	40	40	□	□
666	**226**	1s 6d multicoloured	1·00	1·00	□	□
		p. Phosphor	4·00	4·25	□	□
	Set of 2 (Ordinary)		1·10	1·10	□	□
	Set of 2 (Phosphor)		4·25	4·25	□	□
	First Day Cover (Ordinary)		16·00		□	
	First Day Cover (Phosphor)		18·00		□	

227 Lister's Carbolic Spray

228 Lister and Chemical Symbols

Centenary of Joseph Lister's Discovery of Antiseptic Surgery

1965 (1 SEPT.)

667	**227**	4d indigo, chestnut and grey	10	10	□	□
		p. Phosphor	15	20	□	□
668	**228**	1s black, purple and blue	1·00	1·25	□	□
		p. Phosphor	1·60	1·60	□	□
	Set of 2 (Ordinary)		1·10	1·25	□	□
	Set of 2 (Phosphor)		1·75	1·75	□	□
	First Day Cover (Ordinary)		7·00		□	
	First Day Cover (Phosphor)		7·00		□	

229 Trinidad Carnival Dancers   **230** Canadian Folk-dancers

Commonwealth Arts Festival

1965 (1 Sept.)

669	**229**	6d black and orange		10	10	☐	☐
		p. Phosphor		20	20	☐	☐
670	**230**	1s 6d black and violet		1·40	1·40	☐	☐
		p. Phosphor		1·40	1·40	☐	☐
		Set of 2 (Ordinary)		1·50	1·50	☐	☐
		Set of 2 (Phosphor)		1·60	1·60	☐	☐
		First Day Cover (Ordinary)			8·00		☐
		First Day Cover (Phosphor)			9·00		☐

231 Flight of Spitfires   **232** Pilot in Hurricane

233 Wing-tips of Spitfire and Messerschmitt 'ME-109'   **234** Spitfires attacking Heinkel 'HE-111' Bomber

235 Spitfire attacking Stuka Dive-bomber   **236** Hurricanes over Wreck of Dornier 'DO-17z2' Bomber

The above were issued together *se-tenant* in blocks of six (3 × 2) within the sheet.

237 Anti-aircraft Artillery in Action   **238** Air-battle over St Paul's Cathedral

25th Anniversary of Battle of Britain

1965 (13 Sept.)

671	**231**	4d olive and black		30	35	☐	☐
	a.	*Block of 6*					
		Nos. 671/6	..	5·00	5·00	☐	☐
	p.	*Phosphor*		40	50	☐	☐
	pa.	*Block of 6*					
		Nos. 671p/6p		8·50	8·00	☐	☐
672	**232**	4d olive, blackish olive and black		30	35	☐	☐
	p.	*Phosphor*		40	50	☐	☐
673	**233**	4d multicoloured	..	30	35	☐	☐
	p.	*Phosphor*		40	50	☐	☐
674	**234**	4d olive and black		30	35	☐	☐
	p.	*Phosphor*		40	50	☐	☐
675	**235**	4d olive and black		30	35	☐	☐
	p.	*Phosphor*		40	50	☐	☐
676	**236**	4d multicoloured		30	35	☐	☐
	p.	*Phosphor*		40	50	☐	☐
677	**237**	9d violet, orange and purple		1·25	1·25	☐	☐
	p.	*Phosphor*		80	80	☐	☐
678	**238**	1s 3d multicoloured		1·25	1·25	☐	☐
	p.	*Phosphor*		80	80	☐	☐
		Set of 8 (Ordinary)		6·50	4·25	☐	☐
		Set of 8 (Phosphor)	..	9·00	4·25	☐	☐
		First Day Cover (Ordinary)	..		12·00		☐
		First Day Cover (Phosphor)			15·00		☐
		Presentation Pack (Ordinary)		42·00			☐

239 Tower and Georgian Buildings   **240** Tower and 'Nash' Terrace, Regent's Park

Opening of Post Office Tower

1965 (8 Oct.)

679	**239**	3d yellow, blue and green	..	10	10	☐	☐
		p. Phosphor	..	10	10	☐	☐
680	**240**	1s 3d green and blue		65	75	☐	☐
		p. Phosphor		50	50	☐	☐
		Set of 2 (Ordinary)	..	75	85	☐	☐
		Set of 2 (Phosphor)	..	60	60	☐	☐
		First Day Cover (Ordinary)			4·00		☐
		First Day Cover (Phosphor)			5·00		☐
		Presentation Pack (Ordinary)		1·25			☐
		Presentation Pack (Phosphor)		1·25			☐

241 U.N. Emblem **242** I.C.Y. Emblem

20th Anniversary of UNO and International Co-operation Year

1965 (25 Oct.)

681	241	3d blk, orge & bl ..	15	20	□	□
		p. Phosphor ..	15	20	□	□
682	242	1s 6d blk, pur & bl	1·10	90	□	□
		p. Phosphor	1·10	90	□	□
		Set of 2 (Ordinary) ..	1·25	1·10	□	□
		Set of 2 (Phosphor) ..	1·25	1·10	□	□
		First Day Cover (Ordinary) ..		8·00		□
		First Day Cover (Phosphor)		7·00		□

243 Telecommunications Network **244** Radio Waves and Switchboard

I.T.U. Centenary

1965 (15 Nov.)

683	243	9d multicoloured ..	20	20	□	□
		p. Phosphor ..	60	50	□	□
684	244	1s 6d multicoloured ..	1·40	1·10	□	□
		p. Phosphor ..	6·00	6·00	□	□
		Set of 2 (Ordinary) ..	1·50	1·25	□	□
		Set of 2 (Phosphor) ..	6·50	6·50	□	□
		First Day Cover (Ordinary) ..		7·00		□
		First Day Cover (Phosphor)		9·00		□

245 Robert Burns (after Skirving chalk drawing) **246** Robert Burns (after Nasmyth portrait)

Burns Commemoration

1966 (25 Jan.)

685	245	4d blk, indigo & bl ..	15	15	□	□
		p. Phosphor	15	15	□	□
686	246	1s 3d blk, bl & orge	70	70	□	□
		p. Phosphor	85	85	□	□
		Set of 2 (Ordinary) ..	85	85	□	□
		Set of 2 (Phosphor) ..	1·00	1·00	□	□
		First Day Cover (Ordinary) ..		2·00		□
		First Day Cover (Phosphor)		2·50		□
		Presentation Pack (Ordinary)	16·00			□

247 Westminster Abbey **248** Fan Vaulting, Henry VII Chapel

900th Anniversary of Westminster Abbey

1966 (28 Feb.) *Perf 15 × 14 (3d) or 11 × 12 (2s 6d)*

687	247	3d black, brown and blue ..	15	10	□	□
		p. Phosphor ..	30	30	□	□
688	248	2s 6d black	70	75	□	□
		Set of 2	85	75	□	□
		First Day Cover (Ordinary) ..		4·00		□
		First Day Cover (Phosphor)		6·00		□
		Presentation Pack (Ordinary)	12·00			□

249 View near Hassocks, Sussex **250** Antrim, Northern Ireland

251 Harlech Castle, Wales **252** Cairngorm Mountains, Scotland

Landscapes

1966 (2 May)

689	249	4d black, yellow-green and blue	15	15	□	□
		p. Phosphor ..	15	15	□	□
690	250	6d black, green and blue ..	15	15	□	□
		p. Phosphor ..	25	25	□	□
691	251	1s 3d black, yellow and blue ..	35	35	□	□
		p. Phosphor ..	35	35	□	□
692	252	1s 6d black, orange and blue ..	50	50	□	□
		p. Phosphor ..	50	50	□	□
		Set of 4 (Ordinary)	1·00	1·00	□	□
		Set of 4 (Phosphor)	1·00	1·00	□	□
		First Day Cover (Ordinary)		5·00		□
		First Day Cover (Phosphor)		6·00		□

253 Players with Ball

260 Cup Winners

254 Goalmouth Mêlée

255 Goalkeeper saving Goal

World Cup Football Competition

1966 (1 June)

693	**253**	4d multicoloured ..		15	10	☐	☐
		p. Phosphor	..	15	10	☐	☐
694	**254**	6d multicoloured ..		20	20	☐	☐
		p. Phosphor	..	20	20	☐	☐
695	**255**	1s 3d multicoloured ..		50	50	☐	☐
		p. Phosphor	..	50	50	☐	☐
		Set of 3 (Ordinary)	.. ..	75	75		☐
		Set of 3 (Phosphor)	.. ..	75	75		☐
		First Day Cover (Ordinary) ..			5·00		☐
		First Day Cover (Phosphor)			5·00		☐
		Presentation Pack (Ordinary)			7·50		☐

256 Black-headed Gull

257 Blue Tit

258 Robin

259 Blackbird

The above were issued *se-tenant* in blocks of four within the sheet.

British Birds

1966 (8 Aug.)

696	**256**	4d multicoloured ..		10	15	☐	☐
		a. Block of 4					
		Nos. 696/9	..	90	90	☐	☐
		p. Phosphor	..	10	15	☐	☐
		pa. Block of 4					
		Nos. 696p/9p ..		90	90	☐	☐
697	**257**	4d multicoloured ..		10	15	☐	☐
		p. Phosphor	..	10	15	☐	☐
698	**258**	4d multicoloured ..		10	15	☐	☐
		p. Phosphor	..	10	15	☐	☐
699	**259**	4d multicoloured ..		10	15	☐	☐
		p. Phosphor	..	10	15	☐	☐
		Set of 4 (Ordinary)	.. ..	90	50		☐
		Set of 4 (Phosphor)	.. ..	90	50		☐
		First Day Cover (Ordinary) ..			6·00		☐
		First Day Cover (Phosphor)			5·00		☐
		Presentation Pack (Ordinary)	4·00				☐

England's World Cup Football Victory

1966 (18 Aug.)

700	**260**	4d multicoloured ..		20	20	☐	☐
		First Day Cover	.. ..		1·00		☐

261 Jodrell Bank Radio Telescope

262 British Motor-cars

263 SR N6 Hovercraft

264 Windscale Reactor

British Technology

1966 (19 Sept.)

701	**261**	4d black and lemon		15	15	☐	☐
		p. Phosphor	..	15	15	☐	☐
702	**262**	6d red, blue and					
		orange ..	..	15	15	☐	☐
		p. Phosphor	..	15	15	☐	☐
703	**263**	1s 3d multicoloured ..		30	40	☐	☐
		p. Phosphor	..	35	40	☐	☐
704	**264**	1s 6d multicoloured ..		40	45	☐	☐
		p. Phosphor	..	45	50	☐	☐
		Set of 4 (Ordinary)	..	90	1·00	☐	☐
		Set of 4 (Phosphor)	..	1·00	1·10	☐	☐
		First Day Cover (Ordinary) ..			2·00		☐
		First Day Cover (Phosphor)			2·40		☐
		Presentation Pack (Ordinary)	4·00				☐

265

266

267

268

269

270

The above show battle scenes, they were issued together *se-tenant* in horizontal strips of six within the sheet.

271 Norman Ship

272 Norman Horsemen attacking Harold's Troops

900th Anniversary of Battle of Hastings

1966 (14 Oct.) *Designs show scenes from Bayeux Tapestry.* **Wmk 179** (*sideways on* 1s 3d)

705	265	4d multicoloured ..	10	15	☐	☐
		a. Strip of 6				
		Nos. 705/10	1·50	2·00	☐	☐
		p. Phosphor ..	10	25	☐	☐
		pa. Strip of 6				
		Nos. 705p/10p	1·50	2·00	☐	☐
706	266	4d multicoloured ..	10	15	☐	☐
		p. Phosphor ..	10	25	☐	☐
707	267	4d multicoloured ..	10	15	☐	☐
		p. Phosphor ..	10	25	☐	☐
708	268	4d multicoloured ..	10	15	☐	☐
		p. Phosphor ..	10	25	☐	☐
709	269	4d multicoloured ..	10	15	☐	☐
		p. Phosphor ..	10	25	☐	☐
710	270	4d multicoloured ..	10	15	☐	☐
		p. Phosphor ..	10	25	☐	☐
711	271	6d multicoloured ..	10	10	☐	☐
		p. Phosphor ..	10	10	☐	☐
712	272	1s 3d multicoloured ..	20	20	☐	☐
		p. Phosphor ..	20	20	☐	☐
		Set of 8 (Ordinary) ..	1·60	1·10	☐	☐
		Set of 8 (Phosphor) ..	1·60	1·60	☐	☐
		First Day Cover (Ordinary)		2·50	☐	
		First Day Cover (Phosphor)		2·50	☐	
		Presentation Pack (Ordinary)	3·25		☐	

273 King of the Orient

274 Snowman

Christmas

1966 (1 Dec.) **Wmk 179** (*upright on* 1s 6d)

713	273	3d multicoloured ..	10	10	☐	☐
		p. Phosphor ..	10	10	☐	☐
714	274	1s 6d multicoloured ..	35	35	☐	☐
		p. Phosphor ..	35	35	☐	☐
		Set of 2 (Ordinary) ..	45	45	☐	☐
		Set of 2 (Phosphor) ..	45	45	☐	☐
		First Day Cover (Ordinary)		1·00	☐	
		First Day Cover (Phosphor)		1·00	☐	
		Presentation Pack (Ordinary)	3·00		☐	

275 Sea Freight

276 Air Freight

European Free Trade Association (EFTA)

1967 (20 Feb.)

715	275	9d multicoloured ..	15	15	☐	☐
		p. Phosphor ..	15	15	☐	☐
716	276	1s 6d multicoloured ..	30	30	☐	☐
		p. Phosphor ..	30	30	☐	☐
		Set of 2 (Ordinary) ..	40	40	☐	☐
		Set of 2 (Phosphor) ..	40	40	☐	☐
		First Day Cover (Ordinary)		1·00	☐	
		First Day Cover (Phosphor)		1·00	☐	
		Presentation Pack (Ordinary)	1·25		☐	

277 Hawthorn and Bramble

278 Larger Bindweed and Viper's Bugloss

279 Ox-eye Daisy, Coltsfoot and Buttercup

280 Bluebell, Red Campion and Wood Anemone

The above were issued together *se-tenant* in blocks of four within the sheet.

281 Dog Violet

282 Primroses

British Wild Flowers

1967 (24 APR.)

717	**277**	4d multicoloured ..	15	10	□	□
	a.	*Block of 4*				
		Nos. 717/20 ..	1·00	1·10	□	□
	p.	*Phosphor* ..	10	10	□	□
	pa.	*Block of 4*				
		Nos. 717p/20p	70	80	□	□
718	**278**	4d multicoloured ..	15	10	□	□
	p.	*Phosphor* ..	10	10	□	□
719	**279**	4d multicoloured ..	15	10	□	□
	p.	*Phosphor* ..	10	10	□	□
720	**280**	4d multicoloured ..	15	10	□	□
	p.	*Phosphor* ..	10	10	□	□
721	**281**	9d multicoloured ..	15	10	□	□
	p.	*Phosphor* ..	10	10	□	□
722	**282**	1s 9d multicoloured ..	20	20	□	□
	p.	*Phosphor* ..	30	20	□	□
		Set of 6 (Ordinary)	1·25	65	□	□
		Set of 6 (Phosphor)	1·00	65	□	□
		First Day Cover (Ordinary)		2·00		□
		First Day Cover (Phosphor)		1·60		□
		Presentation Pack·(Ordinary)	2·00		□	

PRESENTATION PACKS IN FOREIGN LANGUAGES

German Presentation Packs are similar to the English versions but have the text printed in German. From the 1969 Collectors Pack until the end of 1974 they were replaced by separately printed insert cards in German. Similar cards in Japanese and Dutch were available from 1969 British Ships issue until end of 1974. A pack printed in Japanese was, however, issued for the 1972 Royal Silver Wedding set.

283 (value at left)   **284** (value at right)

 I   II

Two types of the 2d.

I. Value spaced away from left side of stamp.

II. Value close to left side from new multi-positive. This results in the portrait appearing in the centre, thus conforming with the other values.

1967–69 *Two phosphor bands, except where otherwise stated. No wmk*

723	**283**	½d orange-brown	10	20	□	□
724		1d olive (2 bands)	10	10	□	□
725		1d olive (1 centre band)	25	30	□	□
726		2d lake-brown (Type I) (2 bands)	10	15	□	□
727		2d lake-brown (Type II) (2 bands)	15	15	□	□
728		2d lake-brown (Type II) (1 centre band) ..	40	50	□	□
729		3d violet (1 centre band)	10	10	□	□
730		3d violet (2 bands)	30	30	□	□
731		4d sepia (2 bands)	10	10	□	□
732		4d olive-brown (1 centre band) ..	10	10	□	□
733		4d vermilion (1 centre band) ..	10	10	□	□
734		4d vermilion (1 side band) ..	1·40	1·60	□	□
735		5d blue	10	10	□	□
736		6d purple	20	20	□	□
737	**284**	7d emerald	40	30	□	□
738		8d vermilion	15	30	□	□
739		8d turquoise-blue	45	50	□	□
740		9d green	50	30	□	□
741	**283**	10d drab	45	50	□	□
742		1s violet	40	30	□	□
743		1s 6d blue & dp blue ..	50	30	□	□
	b.	*Phosphorised paper*	75	90	□	□
744		1s 9d orange & black	40	30	□	□
		Set of 16 (one of each value and colour)	3·00	3·25	□	□
		Presentation Pack (one of each value)	6·00		□	
		Presentation Pack (German)	40·00		□	

No. 734 exists with the phosphor band at the left or right. For prices of First Day Covers and for listing of decimal issue, Nos. X841/X1020, see pages 32/6.

285 'Master Lambton'
(Sir Thomas Lawrence)

286 'Mares and Foals in a
Landscape' (George Stubbs)

287 'Children Coming Out
of School' (L. S. Lowry)

288 Gipsy Moth IV

British Paintings

1967 (10 JULY) *Two phosphor bands. No wmk*

748	**285**	4d multicoloured ..	10	10	☐	☐
749	**286**	9d multicoloured ..	20	20	☐	☐
750	**287**	1s 6d multicoloured ..	35	25	☐	☐
	Set of 3		50	50	☐	☐
	First Day Cover		1·10		☐
	Presentation Pack	3·00			☐

Sir Francis Chichester's World Voyage

1967 (24 JULY) *Three phosphor bands. No wmk*

751	**288**	1s 9d multicoloured ..	25	25	☐	☐
	First Day Cover		50		☐

289 Radar Screen

290 Penicillin Mould

291 'VC-10' Jet Engines

292 Television Equipment

British Discovery and Invention

1967 (19 SEPT.) *Two phosphor bands (except 4d, three
bands). Wmk* **179** *(sideways on* 1s 9d)

752	**289**	4d yell, blk & verm ..	10	10	☐	☐
753	**290**	1s multicoloured ..	10	10	☐	☐
754	**291**	1s 6d multicoloured ..	25	15	☐	☐
755	**292**	1s 9d multicoloured ..	30	20	☐	☐
	Set of 4		60	50	☐	☐
	First Day Cover		80		☐
	Presentation Pack	1·50			☐

NO WATERMARK. All the following issues are on un-
watermarked paper unless stated.

293 'The Adoration of
the Shepherds'
(School of Seville)

294 'Madonna and
Child' (Murillo)

295 'The Adoration of the Shepherds'
(Louis Le Nain)

Christmas

1967 *Two phosphor bands (except 3d, one phosphor band)*

756	**293**	3d multicoloured (27 Nov.) ..	10	10	☐	☐
757	**294**	4d multicoloured (18 Oct.) ..	10	10	☐	☐
758	**295**	1s 6d multicoloured (27 Nov.) ..	35	35	☐	☐
	Set of 3		50	50	☐	☐
	First Day Covers (2)		1·00		☐

Gift Pack 1967

1967 (27 Nov.) *Comprises Nos.* 715p/22p *and* 748/58

	Gift Pack	2·50	☐

1967–68 *No wmk* *Perf* 11×12

759	**166**	2s 6d brown	40	50	☐	☐
760	**167**	5s red	1·00	1·00	☐	☐
761	**168**	10s blue	5·00	5·50	☐	☐
762	**169**	£1 black	4·00	4·00	☐	☐
	Set of 4	9·00	10·00	☐	☐

296 Tarr Steps, Exmoor

297 Aberfeldy Bridge

298 Menai Bridge

299 M4 Viaduct

British Bridges

1968 (29 Apr.) *Two phosphor bands*

763	**296**	4d multicoloured ..	10	10	☐	☐
764	**297**	9d multicoloured ..	10	10	☐	☐
765	**298**	1s 6d multicoloured ..	20	15	☐	☐
766	**299**	1s 9d multicoloured ..	25	30	☐	☐
		Set of 4	60	60	☐	☐
		First Day Cover		1·10		☐
		Presentation Pack	1·25		☐	

300 'TUC' and Trades Unionists

301 Mrs Emmeline Pankhurst (statue)

302 Sopwith 'Camel' and 'Lightning' Fighters

303 Captain Cook's *Endeavour* and Signature

British Anniversaries. Events described on stamps

1968 (29 May) *Two phosphor bands*

767	**300**	4d multicoloured ..	10	10	☐	☐
768	**301**	9d violet, grey and black	10	10	☐	☐
769	**302**	1s multicoloured ..	20	20	☐	☐
770	**303**	1s 9d ochre and brown	25	25	☐	☐
		Set of 4	60	60	☐	☐
		First Day Cover		3·25		☐
		Presentation Pack	1·60		☐	

304 'Queen Elizabeth I' (Unknown Artist)

305 'Pinkie' (Lawrence)

306 'Ruins of St Mary Le Port' (Piper)

307 'The Hay Wain' (Constable)

British Paintings

1968 (12 Aug.) *Two phosphor bands*

771	**304**	4d multicoloured ..	10	10	☐	☐
772	**305**	1s multicoloured ..	15	15	☐	☐
773	**306**	1s 6d multicoloured ..	20	20	☐	☐
774	**307**	1s 9d multicoloured ..	25	25	☐	☐
		Set of 4	60	60	☐	☐
		First Day Cover		1·00		☐
		Presentation Pack	1·40		☐	
		Presentation Pack (German)	6·00		☐	

Gift Pack 1968

1968 (16 Sept.) *Comprises Nos. 763/74*

Gift Pack	7·00		☐
Gift Pack (German)	18·00		☐

Collectors Pack 1968

1968 (16 Sept.) *Comprises Nos. 752/8 and 763/74*

Collectors Pack	6·00	☐

308 Girl and Boy with Rocking Horse

309 Girl with Doll's House

310 Boy with Train Set

Christmas

1968 (25 Nov.) *Two phosphor bands (except 4d, one centre phosphor band)*

775	**308**	4d multicoloured ..	10	10	☐	☐
776	**309**	9d multicoloured ..	15	15	☐	☐
777	**310**	1s 6d multicoloured ..	25	25	☐	☐
	Set of 3	.. .. ..	50	50	☐	☐
	First Day Cover			60	☐
	Presentation Pack	1·40			☐
	Presentation Pack (German)	6·00			☐

311 RMS *Queen Elizabeth 2*

312 Elizabethan Galleon

313 East Indiaman

314 *Cutty Sark*

315 SS *Great Britain*

The 9d and 1s values were arranged in horizontal strips of three and pairs respectively throughout the sheet.

316 RMS *Mauretania*

British Ships

1969 (15 Jan.) *Two phosphor bands (except 5d, one horiz phosphor band, 1s, two vert phosphor bands at right)*

778	**311**	5d multicoloured ..	10	10	☐	☐
779	**312**	9d multicoloured ..	10	15	☐	☐
		a. Strip of 3				
		Nos. 779/81 ..	85	85	☐	☐
780	**313**	9d multicoloured ..	10	15	☐	☐
781	**314**	9d multicoloured ..	10	15	☐	☐
782	**315**	1s multicoloured ..	25	25	☐	☐
		a. Pair. Nos. 782/3	90	85	☐	☐
783	**316**	1s multicoloured ..	25	25	☐	☐
	Set of 6		1·60	90	☐	☐
	First Day Cover			3·25	☐
	Presentation Pack		2·50		☐
	Presentation Pack (German)	22·00			☐

317 'Concorde' in Flight

318 Plan and Elevation Views

319 'Concorde's' Nose and Tail

320 (See also Type **359a**)

First Flight of 'Concorde'

1969 (3 Mar.) *Two phosphor bands*

784	**317**	4d multicoloured ..	10	10	☐	☐
785	**318**	9d multicoloured ..	20	20	☐	☐
786	**319**	1s 6d deep blue, grey				
		and light blue ..	30	30	☐	☐
	Set of 3		50	50	☐	☐
	First Day Cover			80	☐
	Presentation Pack		2·00		☐
	Presentation Pack (German)	18·00			☐

1969 (5 Mar.) *P 12*

787	**320**	2s 6d brown	50	30	☐	☐
788		5s lake	2·00	60	☐	☐
789		10s ultramarine ..	7·00	7·50	☐	☐
790		£1 black	3·00	1·60	☐	☐
	Set of 4		11·00	9·00	☐	☐
	Presentation Pack		18·00		☐
	Presentation Pack (German)	45·00			☐

321 Page from the *Daily Mail*, and Vickers 'Vimy' Aircraft

322 Europa and C.E.P.T. Emblems

323 I.L.O. Emblem

324 Flags of N.A.T.O. Countries

325 Vickers 'Vimy' Aircraft and Globe showing Flight

Anniversaries. Events described on stamps

1969 (2 APR.) Two phosphor bands

791	321	5d multicoloured ..		10	10	☐	☐
792	322	9d multicoloured ..		20	20	☐	☐
793	323	1s claret, red and					
		blue	.. ..	20	20	☐	☐
794	324	1s 6d multicoloured ..		20	20	☐	☐
795	325	1s 9d olive, yellow and					
		turquoise-green		25	25	☐	☐
		Set of 5		85	85	☐	☐
		First Day Cover			1·25	☐	
		Presentation Pack		2·25		☐	
		Presentation Pack (German)		40·00		☐	

326 Durham Cathedral

327 York Minster

328 St Giles' Cathedral, Edinburgh

329 Canterbury Cathedral

The above were issued together *se-tenant* in blocks of four within the sheet.

330 St Paul's Cathedral

331 Liverpool Metropolitan Cathedral

British Architecture (Cathedrals)

1969 (28 MAY) Two phosphor bands

796	326	5d multicoloured ..		10	10	☐	☐
	a	Block of 4					
		Nos. 796/9 ..		85	1·00	☐	☐
797	327	5d multicoloured ..		10	10	☐	☐
798	328	5d multicoloured ..		10	10	☐	☐
799	329	5d multicoloured ..		10	10	☐	☐
800	330	9d multicoloured ..		15	15	☐	☐
801	331	1s 6d multicoloured ..		15	15	☐	☐
		Set of 6		1·00	55	☐	☐
		First Day Cover			1·75	☐	
		Presentation Pack		2·40		☐	
		Presentation Pack (German)		22·00		☐	

332 The King's Gate, Caernarvon Castle

333 The Eagle Tower, Caernarvon Castle

334 Queen Eleanor's Gate, Caernarvon Castle

335 Celtic Cross, Margam Abbey

The 5d values were printed *se-tenant* in strips of three throughout the sheet.

336 Prince Charles

337 Mahatma Gandhi

Investiture of H.R.H. The Prince of Wales

1969 (1 JULY) *Two phosphor bands*

802	**332**	5d multicoloured ..	10	10	☐	☐
		a. Strip of 3				
		Nos. 802/4	70	75	☐	☐
803	**333**	5d multicoloured ..	10	10	☐	☐
804	**334**	5d multicoloured ..	10	10	☐	☐
805	**335**	9d multicoloured ..	20	10	☐	☐
806	**336**	1s black and gold ..	20	10	☐	☐
		Set of 5	1·00	45	☐	☐
		First Day Cover		1·00		☐
		Presentation Pack	1·40			☐
		Presentation Pack (German)	16·00			☐

Gandhi Centenary Year

1969 (13 AUG.) *Two phosphor bands*

807	**337**	1s 6d multicoloured ..	30	30	☐	☐
		First Day Cover		50		☐

Collectors Pack 1969

1969 (15 SEPT.) *Comprises Nos. 775/86 and 791/807*

	Collectors Pack	22·00	☐

338 National Giro

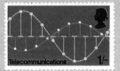

339 Telecommunications

340 Telecommunications

341 Automatic Sorting

British Post Office Technology

1969 (1 OCT.) *Two phosphor bands*   *Perf* 13½×14

808	**338**	5d multicoloured ..	10	10	☐	☐
809	**339**	9d green, bl & blk ..	15	15	☐	☐
810	**340**	1s green, lav & blk ..	15	15	☐	☐
811	**341**	1s 6d multicoloured ..	40	40	☐	☐
		Set of 4	70	70	☐	☐
		First Day Cover		1·00		☐
		Presentation Pack	2·25			☐

342 Herald Angel

343 The Three Shepherds

344 The Three Kings

Christmas

1969 (26 NOV.) *Two phosphor bands (5d, 1s 6d) or one centre band (4d)*

812	**342**	4d multicoloured ..	10	10	☐	☐
813	**343**	5d multicoloured ..	10	10	☐	☐
814	**344**	1s 6d multicoloured ..	30	30	☐	☐
		Set of 3	45	45	☐	☐
		First Day Cover		50		☐
		Presentation Pack	2·25			☐

345 Fife Harling

346 Cotswold Limestone

347 Welsh Stucco

348 Ulster Thatch

British Rural Architecture

1970 (11 FEB.) *Two phosphor bands*

815	**345**	5d multicoloured ..	10	10	☐	☐
816	**346**	9d multicoloured ..	20	20	☐	☐
817	**347**	1s multicoloured ..	20	20	☐	☐
818	**348**	1s 6d multicoloured ..	35	35	☐	☐
		Set of 4	75	75	☐	☐
		First Day Cover		1·00		☐
		Presentation Pack	2·25			☐

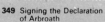

349 Signing the Declaration of Arbroath

350 Florence Nightingale attending Patients

351 Signing of International Co-operative Alliance

352 Pilgrims and *Mayflower*

353 Sir William Herschel, Francis Baily, Sir John Herschel and Telescope

Anniversaries. Events described on stamps

1970 (1 APR.) *Two phosphor bands*

819	**349**	5d multicoloured ..	10	10	□	□
820	**350**	9d multicoloured ..	15	15	□	□
821	**351**	1s multicoloured ..	25	15	□	□
822	**352**	1s 6d multicoloured ..	30	30	□	□
823	**353**	1s 9d multicoloured ..	30	30	□	□
		Set of 5	1·00	90	□	□
		First Day Cover		1·25	□	
		Presentation Pack ..	2·25		□	

354 'Mr Pickwick and Sam' (*Pickwick Papers*)

355 'Mr and Mrs Micawber' (*David Copperfield*)

356 'David Copperfield and Betsy Trotwood' (*David Copperfield*)

357 'Oliver asking for more' (*Oliver Twist*)

The 5d values were issued together *se-tenant* in blocks of four within the sheet.

358 'Grasmere' (from engraving by J. Farrington, R.A.)

Literary Anniversaries. Events described on stamps

1970 (3 JUNE) *Two phosphor bands*

824	**354**	5d multicoloured ..	10	10	□	□
		a. Block of 4				
		Nos. 824/7 ..	90	90	□	□
825	**355**	5d multicoloured ..	10	10	□	□
826	**356**	5d multicoloured ..	10	10	□	□
827	**357**	5d multicoloured ..	10	10	□	□
828	**358**	1s 6d multicoloured ..	20	20	□	□
		Set of 5	1·00	55	□	□
		First Day Cover ..		1·50	□	
		Presentation Pack ..	2·25		□	

359

359a (Value redrawn)

Decimal Currency

1970 (17 JUNE)—72 *10p and some printings of the* 50p *were issued on phosphor paper* Perf 12

829	**359**	10p cerise	1·00	75	□	□
830		20p olive-green ..	70	15	□	□
831		50p ultramarine ..	1·40	40	□	□
831b	**359a**	£1 black	2·75	75	□	□
		Set of 4	5·25	1·75	□	□
829/31		Presentation Pack ..	7·00		□	
790 (or 831b), 830/1						
		Presentation Pack ..	8·00		□	

For First Day Cover prices see page 36.

360 Runners

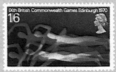

361 Swimmers

362 Cyclists

Ninth British Commonwealth Games

1970 (15 JULY) *Two phosphor bands* *Perf* $13\frac{1}{2} \times 14$

832	**360**	5d	pink, emerald, greenish yellow & yellow-green	10	10	☐	☐
833	**361**	1s 6d	greenish blue, lilac, brown and Prussian blue ..	40	40	☐	☐
834	**362**	1s 9d	yellow-orange, lilac, salmon and red-brown ..	40	40	☐	☐
		Set of 3	.. ..	80	80	☐	☐
		First Day Cover	.. .. ..		80		☐
		Presentation Pack	.. .. ..	2·00			☐

Collectors Pack 1970

1970 (14 SEPT.) *Comprises Nos. 808/28 and 832/4*

	Collectors Pack	.. .. ..	26·00	☐

363 1d Black (1840)

364 1s Green (1847)

365 4d Carmine (1855)

'Philympia 70' Stamp Exhibition

1970 (18 SEPT.) *Two phosphor bands* *Perf* $14 \times 14\frac{1}{2}$

835	**363**	5d	multicoloured ..	10	10	☐	☐
836	**364**	9d	multicoloured ..	35	35	☐	☐
837	**365**	1s 6d	multicoloured ..	40	40	☐	☐
		Set of 3	.. .. ..	75	75	☐	☐
		First Day Cover	.. ..		1·00		☐
		Presentation Pack	.. ..	1·90			☐

366 Shepherds and Apparition of the Angel

367 Mary, Joseph, and Christ in the Manger

368 The Wise Men bearing Gifts

Christmas

1970 (25 NOV.) *Two phosphor bands* (5d, 1s 6d) *or one centre phosphor band* (4d)

838	**366**	4d	multicoloured ..	10	10	☐	☐
839	**367**	5d	multicoloured ..	10	10	☐	☐
840	**368**	1s 6d	multicoloured ..	35	35	☐	☐
		Set of 3	.. .. ..	50	50	☐	☐
		First Day Cover ..			60		☐
		Presentation Pack	.. ..	2·00			☐

369

369a

Decimal Currency
1971–90. *Type* **369**

(a) *Printed in photogravure by Harrison and Sons with phosphor bands. Perf* 15×14

X841	$\frac{1}{2}$p	turq-bl (2 bands) ..	10	10	☐ ☐
X842	$\frac{1}{2}$p	turq-bl (1 side band) ..	65·00	25·00	☐ ☐
X843	$\frac{1}{2}$p	turquoise-blue (1 centre band)	20	20	☐ ☐
X844	1p	crimson (2 bands) ..	10	10	☐ ☐
X845	1p	crim (1 centre band) ..	20	20	☐ ☐
X846	1p	crimson ('all-over' phosphor)	20	20	☐ ☐
X847	1p	crimson (1 side band) ..	75	90	☐ ☐
X848	$1\frac{1}{2}$p	black (2 bands)	20	15	☐ ☐
X849	2p	myr-grn (face value as in T **369**) (2 bands) ..	20	10	☐ ☐
X850	2p	myr-grn (face value as in T **369**) 'all-over' phosphor ..	20	15	☐ ☐
X851	$2\frac{1}{2}$p	mag (1 centre band) ..	15	10	☐ ☐
X852	$2\frac{1}{2}$p	magenta (1 side band)	1·75	1·75	☐ ☐
X853	$2\frac{1}{2}$p	magenta (2 bands) ..	20	30	☐ ☐
X854	$2\frac{1}{2}$p	rose-red (2 bands) ..	40	40	☐ ☐
X855	3p	ultramarine (2 bands)	20	10	☐ ☐
X856	3p	ultram (1 centre band)	20	25	☐ ☐
X857	3p	bright magenta (2 bands)	30	25	☐ ☐
X858	$3\frac{1}{2}$p	olive-grey (2 bands) ..	30	30	☐ ☐
X859	$3\frac{1}{2}$p	ol-grey (1 centre band)	30	15	☐ ☐

X860	3½p purple-brown (1 centre band)	1·75	1·25	☐	☐
X861	4p ochre-brown (2 bands)	20	20	☐	☐
X862	4p greenish bl (2 bands)	2·00	1·75	☐	☐
X863	4p greenish blue (1 centre band)	75	75	☐	☐
X864	4p greenish blue (1 side band)	1·25	1·50	☐	☐
X865	4½p grey-blue (2 bands)	20	25	☐	☐
X866	5p pale violet (2 bands)	20	10	☐	☐
X867	5p claret (1 centre band)	90	1·00	☐	☐
X868	5½p violet (2 bands)	25	25	☐	☐
X869	5½p violet (1 centre band)	20	20	☐	☐
X870	6p light emerald (2 bands)	30	15	☐	☐
X871	6½p greenish bl (2 bands)	45	45	☐	☐
X872	6½p greenish blue (1 centre band)	30	15	☐	☐
X873	6½p greenish blue (1 side band)	60	55	☐	☐
X874	7p purple-brn (2 bands)	35	25	☐	☐
X875	7p purple-brown (1 centre band)	35	20	☐	☐
X876	7p purple-brown (1 side band)	60	75	☐	☐
X877	7½p chestnut (2 bands)	30	25	☐	☐
X878	8p rosine (2 bands)	25	20	☐	☐
X879	8p rosine (1 centre band)	25	15	☐	☐
X880	8p rosine (1 side band)	50	60	☐	☐
X881	8½p yellowish green (2 bands)	35	20	☐	☐
X882	9p yellow-orange and black (2 bands)	60	30	☐	☐
X883	9p deep violet (2 bands)	45	25	☐	☐
X884	9½p purple (2 bands)	45	30	☐	☐
X885	10p orange-brown and chestnut (2 bands)	40	30	☐	☐
X886	10p orange-brn (2 bands)	40	20	☐	☐
X887	10p orange-brown ('all-over' phosphor)	30	45	☐	☐
X888	10p orange-brown (1 centre band)	30	20	☐	☐
X889	10p orange-brown (1 side band)	60	60	☐	☐
X890	10½p yellow (2 bands)	40	30	☐	☐
X891	10½p blue (2 bands)	60	45	☐	☐
X892	11p brown-red (2 bands)	40	25	☐	☐
X893	11½p drab (1 centre band)	45	30	☐	☐
X894	11½p drab (1 side band)	60	60	☐	☐
X895	12p yellowish green (2 bands)	45	40	☐	☐
X896	12p bright emerald (1 centre band)	60	40	☐	☐
X897	12p bright emerald (1 side band)	75	75	☐	☐
X898	12½p light emerald (1 centre band)	45	25	☐	☐
X899	12½p light emerald (1 side band)	60	60	☐	☐
X900	13p pale chestnut (1 centre band)	50	35	☐	☐
X901	13p pale chestnut (1 side band)	60	60	☐	☐
X902	14p grey-blue (2 bands)	50	45	☐	☐
X903	14p dp bl (1 centre band)	25	30	☐	☐
X904	14p dp blue (1 side band)	25	30	☐	☐
X905	15p brt bl (1 centre band)	25	30	☐	☐
X906	15p brt blue (1 side band)	25	30	☐	☐
X907	15½p pale violet (2 bands)	45	45	☐	☐
X908	16p olive-drab (2 bands)	1·50	1·75	☐	☐
X909	17p grey-blue (2 bands)	75	75	☐	☐
X909m	17p dp bl (1 centre band)	30	35	☐	☐
X909n	17p dp bl (1 side band)	30	35	☐	☐
X910	18p dp ol-grey (2 bands)	75	75	☐	☐
X911	19p bright orange-red (2 bands)	75	75	☐	☐
X912	20p dull purple (2 bands)	75	40	☐	☐
X913	20p brownish black (2 bands)	30	30	☐	☐
X913a	22p bright orange-red (2 bands)	35	45	☐	☐
X914	26p rosine (2 bands)	3·50	3·50	☐	☐
X915	31p purple (2 bands)	3·50	3·50	☐	☐
X916	34p ochre-brown (2 bands)	3·50	3·50	☐	☐
X917	50p ochre-brown (2 bands)	1·75	40	☐	☐
X918	50p ochre (2 bands)	1·90	2·10	☐	☐

(b) Printed in photogravure by Harrison and Sons on phosphorised paper. Perf 15 × 14

X924	½p turquoise-blue	10	10	☐	☐
X925	1p crimson	10	10	☐	☐
X926	2p myrtle-green (face value as in T 369)	10	10	☐	☐
X927	2p deep green (smaller value as in T 369a)	10	10	☐	☐
X928	2p myr-grn (smaller value as in T 369a)	20	10	☐	☐
X929	2½p rose-red	20	20	☐	☐
X930	3p bright magenta	10	10	☐	☐
X931	3½p purple-brown	35	30	☐	☐
X932	4p greenish blue	25	20	☐	☐
X933	4p new blue	10	10	☐	☐
X934	5p pale violet	30	25	☐	☐
X935	5p dull red-brown	10	10	☐	☐
X936	7p red	2·00	1·50	☐	☐
X937	8½p yellowish green	30	55	☐	☐
X938	10p orange-brown	15	20	☐	☐
X938a	10p dull orange	15	20	☐	☐
X939	11p brown-red	60	75	☐	☐
X940	11½p ochre-brown	50	45	☐	☐
X941	12p yellowish green	45	40	☐	☐
X942	13p olive-grey	60	45	☐	☐
X943	13½p purple-brown	65	60	☐	☐
X944	14p grey-blue	50	40	☐	☐
X945	15p ultramarine	50	40	☐	☐
X946	15½p pale violet	50	40	☐	☐
X947	16p olive-drab	60	30	☐	☐
X948	16½p pale chestnut	85	75	☐	☐
X949	17p light emerald	70	40	☐	☐
X950	17p grey-blue	60	40	☐	☐
X951	17½p pale chestnut	80	80	☐	☐
X952	18p deep violet	70	75	☐	☐
X953	18p deep olive-grey	70	60	☐	☐
X954	19p bright orange-red	30	35	☐	☐
X955	19½p olive-grey	2·50	1·50	☐	☐

X956	20p	dull purple	80	20	□	□
X957	20p	turquoise-green ..	30	35	□	□
X958	20p	brownish black ..	30	30	□	□
X959	20½p	ultramarine	1·10	85	□	□
X960	22p	blue	80	45	□	□
X961	22p	bright green	35	45	□	□
X961b	22p	bright orange-red ..	35	45	□	□
X962	23p	brown-red	1·40	60	□	□
X963	23p	bright green ..	35	40	□	□
X964	24p	violet	75	60	□	□
X965	24p	Indian red	40	45	□	□
X966	25p	purple	90	90	□	□
X967	26p	rosine	90	30	□	□
X967b	26p	drab ..	40	45	□	□
X968	27p	chestnut	45	50	□	□
X968n	27p	violet	45	50	□	□
X969	28p	deep violet ..	75	60	□	□
X970	28p	ochre	45	50	□	□
X971	29p	ochre-brown ..	2·50	1·25	□	□
X972	29p	deep mauve ..	45	50	□	□
X973	30p	deep olive-grey ..	45	50	□	□
X974	31p	purple	1·10	80	□	□
X974b	31p	ultramarine ..	50	55	□	□
X975	32p	greenish blue ..	50	55	□	□
X975a	33p	light emerald ..	50	55	□	□
X976	34p	ochre-brown ..	1·10	80	□	□
X977	34p	deep bluish grey ..	55	55	□	□
X978	35p	sepia	55	60	□	□
X979	37p	rosine	60	65	□	□

(c) Printed in photogravure by Harrison and Sons on ordinary paper. Perf 15 × 14

X980	50p	ochre-brown	75	45	□	□
X981	50p	ochre	75	45	□	□
X982	75p	grey-black (smaller values as T **369a**) ..	1·10	1·25	□	□

(d) Printed in lithography by John Waddington. Perf 14

X996	4p	greenish blue (2 bands)	20	25	□	□
X997	4p	greenish blue (phosphorised paper)	25	20	□	□
X998	20p	dull purple (2 bands)	85	40	□	□
X999	20p	dull purple (phosphorised paper)	85	40	□	□

(e) Printed in lithography by Questa. Perf 13½ × 14 (Nos X1000, X1003/4 and X1014) or 15 × 14 (others)

X1000	2p	emerald-green (face value as in T **369**) (phosphorised paper)	20	20	□	□
	a	*Perf* 15 × 14	20	20	□	□
X1001	2p	bright grn and dp grn (smaller value as in T **369a**) (phosphorised paper) ..	25	25	□	□
X1002	4p	greenish blue (phosphorised paper)	20	20	□	□
X1003	5p	light violet (phosphorised paper)	20	20	□	□

X1004	5p	claret (phosphorised paper)	40	20	□	□
	a	*Perf* 15 × 14	25	25	□	□
X1005	13p	pale chest (1 centre band)	60	60	□	□
X1006	13p	pale chest (1 side band)	60	60	□	□
X1007	14p	dp bl (1 centre band) ..	60	50	□	□
X1008	18p	deep olive-grey (phosphorised paper)	60	60	□	□
X1009	18p	dp ol-grey (2 bands)	3·00	2·00	□	□
X1010	19p	bright orange-red (phosphorised paper)	90	75	□	□
X1011	20p	dull purple (phosphorised paper)	75	60	□	□
X1012	22p	yell-grn (2 bands) ..	3·00	2·00	□	□
X1013	34p	ochre-brn (2 bands)	3·00	2·00	□	□
X1014	75p	black (face value as T **369**) (ordinary paper)	2·00	1·50	□	□
	a	*Perf* 15 × 14	2·50	1·50	□	□
X1015	75p	brownish grey and black (smaller value as T **369a**) (ordinary paper)	4·50	1·75	□	□

(f) Printed in lithography by Walsall. Perf 14

X1016	14p	deep blue (1 side band)	1·00	1·00	□	□
X1017	19p	bright orange-red (2 bands)	1·00	1·00	□	□
X1018	29p	deep mauve (2 bands)	45	1·00	□	□
X1019	29p	deep mauve (phosphorised paper)	45	50	□	□
X1020	31p	ultramarine (phosphorised paper)	50	55	□	□

Presentation Pack (contains ½p (X841), 1p (X844), 1½p (X848), 2p (X849), 2½p (X851), 3p (X855), 3½p (X858), 4p (X861), 5p (X866), 6p (X870), 7½p (X877), 9p (X882)) 4·00 □

Presentation Pack ('Scandinavia 71') (contents as above) .. 32·00 □

Presentation Pack (contains ½p (X841), 1p (X844), 1½p (X848), 2p (X849), 2½p (X851), 3p (X855 or X856), 3½p (X858 or X859), 4p (X861), 4½p (X865), 5p (X866), 5½p (X868 or X869), 6p (X870), 6½p (X871 or X872), 7p (X874), 7½p (X877), 8p (X878), 9p (X882), 10p (X885)) .. .. .. 4·00 □

Presentation Pack (contains ½p (X841), 1p (X844), 1½p (X848), 2p (X849), 2½p (X851), 3p (X856), 5p (X866), 6½p (X872), 7p (X874 or X875), 7½p (X877), 8p (X878), 8½p (X881), 9p (X883), 9½p (X884), 10p (X886), 10½p (X890), 11p (X892) 20p (X912), 50p (X917)) .. .. 5·00 □

34

Presentation Pack (contains 2½p
   (X929), 3p (X930), 4p (X996), 10½p
   (X891), 11½p (X893), 11½p (X940),
   12p (X941), 13p (X942), 13½p
   (X943), 14p (X944), 15p (X945),
   15½p (X946), 17p (X949), 17½p
   (X951), 18p (X952), 22p (X960),
   25p (X966), 75p (X1014)) .. .. 12·00 □

Presentation Pack (contains ½p
   (X924), 1p (X925), 2p (X1000), 3p
   (X930), 3½p (X931), 4p (X997), 5p
   (X1004), 10p (X888), 12½p (X898),
   16p (X947), 16½p (X948), 17p
   (X950), 20p (X999), 20½p (X959),
   23p (X962), 26p (X967), 28p
   (X969), 31p (X974), 50p (X980),
   75p (X1014)) .. .. 22·00 □

Presentation Pack (contains ½p
   (X924), 1p (X925), 2p (X1000a),
   3p (X930), 4p (X997), 5p (X1004a),
   10p (X938), 13p (X900), 16p
   (X947), 17p (X950), 18p (X953),
   20p (X999), 22p (X961), 24p
   (X964), 26p (X967), 28p (X969),
   31p (X974), 34p (X976), 50p
   (X980), 75p (X1014a)) .. .. 15·00 □

Presentation Pack (contains 1p
   (X925), 2p (X1000a), 3p (X930),
   4p (X997), 5p (X1004a), 7p (X936),
   10p (X938), 12p (X896), 13p
   (X900), 17p (X950), 18p (X953),
   20p (X999), 22p (X961), 24p
   (X964), 26p (X967), 28p (X969),
   31p (X974), 34p (X976), 50p
   (X980), 75p (X1014a)) .. .. 6·50 □

Presentation Pack (contains 14p
   (X903), 19p (X954), 20p (X957),
   23p (X963), 27p (X968), 28p
   (X970), 32p (X975), 35p (X978)) .. 3·50 □

Presentation Pack (contains 15p
   (X905), 20p (X958), 24p (X965),
   29p (X972), 30p (X973), 34p
   (X977), 37p (X979) .. .. .. 3·25 □

Presentation Pack (contains 10p
   (X938a), 17p (X909m), 22p
   (X961b), 26p (X967b), 27p (X968n),
   31p (X974b), 33p (X975a) .. 2·75 □

"X" NUMBERS. These are provisional only and may be amended in future editions.

PHOSPHOR BANDS. See notes on page 15.
Phosphor bands are applied to the stamps, after the design has been printed, by a separate cylinder. On issues with "all-over" phosphor the "band" covers the entire stamp. Parts of the stamp covered by phosphor bands, or the entire surface for "all-over" phosphor versions, appear matt.
Nos. X847, X852, X864, X873, X876, X880, X889, X894, X897, X899, X901, X906, X909n and X1006 exist with the phosphor band at the left or right of the stamp.

PHOSPHORISED PAPER. First introduced as an experiment for a limited printing of the 1s 6d value (No. 743b) in 1969 this paper has the phosphor, to activate the automatic sorting machinery, added to the paper coating before the stamps were printed. Issues on this paper have a completely shiny surface. Although not adopted after this first trial further experiments on the 8½p in 1976 led to this paper being used for new printings of current values.

QUEEN ELIZABETH II DEFINITIVE FIRST DAY COVERS

The British Post Office did not introduce special First Day of Issue postmarks for definitive issues until the first instalment of the Machin £sd series, issued 5 June 1967, although "First Day" treatment had been provided for some Regional stamps from 8 June 1964 onwards.

1952–1966

PRICES for First Day Covers listed below are for stamps, as indicated, used on illustrated envelopes and postmarked with operational cancellations.

5 Dec. 1952	1½d, 2½d (*Nos.* 517, 519) ..	6·00	☐
6 July 1953	5d, 8d, 1s (*Nos.* 522, 525, 529)	25·00	☐
31 Aug. 1953	½d, 1d, 2d (*Nos.* 515/16, 518)	20·00	☐
2 Nov. 1953	4d, 1s 3d, 1s 6d (*Nos.* 521, 530/1)	50·00	☐
18 Jan. 1954	3d, 6d, 7d (*Nos.* 520, 523/4)	30·00	☐
8 Feb. 1954	9d, 10d, 11d (*Nos.* 526/8) ..	60·00	☐
1 Sept. 1955	10s, £1 (*Nos.* 538/9) ..	£400	☐
23 Sept. 1955	2s 6d, 5s (*Nos.* 536/7) ..	£175	☐
19 Nov. 1957	½d, 1d, 1½d, 2d, 2½d, 3d (*graphite lines*) (*Nos.* 561/6)	60·00	☐
9 Feb. 1959	4½d (*No.* 577)	45·00	☐

1967–1989

PRICES for First Day Covers listed below are for stamps, as indicated, used on illustrated envelopes and postmarked with the special First Day of Issue handstamps. Other definitives issued during this period were not accepted for "First Day" treatment by the British Post Office.

£sd Machin Issues

5 June 1967	4d, 1s, 1s 9d (*Nos.*731,742, 744)	1·40	☐
8 Aug. 1967	3d, 9d, 1s 6d (*Nos.*729,740, 743)	1·40	☐
5 Feb. 1968	½d, 1d, 2d, 6d (*Nos.* 723/4, 726, 736)	75	☐
1 July 1968	5d, 7d, 8d, 10d (*Nos.* 735, 737/8, 741)	1·10	☐
5 March 1969	2s 6d, 5s, 10s, £1 (*Nos.* 787/90)	15·00	☐

Decimal Machin Issues

17 June 1970	10p, 20p, 50p, (*Nos.* 829/31)	5·50	☐
15 Feb. 1971	½p, 1p, 1½p, 2p, 2½p, 3p, 3½p, 4p, 5p, 6p, 7½p, 9p (*Nos.* X841, X844, X848/9, X851, X855, X858, X861, X866, X870, X877, X882) (*Covers carry* "POSTING DELAYED BY THE POST OFFICE STRIKE 1971" *cachet*) ..	2·75	☐
11 Aug. 1971	10p (*No.* X885)	1·00	☐

6 Dec. 1972	£1 (*No.* 831b)	7·00	☐
24 Oct. 1973	4½p, 5½p, 8p, (*Nos.* X865, X868, X878)	1·00	☐
4 Sept. 1974	6½p (*No.* X871)	1·40	☐
15 Jan. 1975	7p (*No.* X874)	75	☐
24 Sept. 1975	8½p (*No.* X881)	1·25	☐
25 Feb. 1976	9p, 9½p, 10p, 10½p, 11p, 20p (*Nos.* X883/4, X886, X890, X892, X912)	2·75	☐
2 Feb. 1977	50p (*No.* X917)	2·25	☐
2 Feb. 1977	£1, £2, £5 (*Nos.* 1026, 1027/8)	12·00	☐
26 April 1978	10½p (*No.* X891)	1·00	☐
15 Aug. 1979	11½p, 13p, 15p (*Nos.* X940, X942, X945)	2·00	☐
30 Jan. 1980	4p, 12p, 13½p, 17p, 17½p, 75p (*Nos.* X996, X941, X943, X949, X951, X1014) ..	4·50	☐
22 Oct. 1980	3p, 22p, (*Nos.* X930, X960)	1·00	☐
14 Jan. 1981	2½p, 11½p, 14p, 15½p, 18p, 25p (*Nos.* X929, X893, X944, X946, X952, X966)	2·25	☐
27 Jan. 1982	5p, 12½p, 16½p, 19½p, 26p, 29p (*Nos.* X1004, X898, X948, X955, X967, X971) ..	3·25	☐
30 March 1983	3½p, 16p, 17p, 20½p, 23p, 28p, 31p, (*Nos.* X931, X947, X950, X959, X962, X969, X974)	6·00	☐
3 Aug. 1983	£1·30 (*No.* 1026b)	10·00	☐
28 Aug. 1984	13p, 18p, 22p, 24p, 34p, (*Nos.* X900, X953, X961, X964, X976)	5·00	☐
28 Aug. 1984	£1·33 (*No.* 1026c)	8·50	☐
17 Sept. 1985	£1·41 (*No.* 1026d)	7·50	☐
29 Oct. 1985	7p, 12p (*No.* X936, X896)	2·00	☐
2 Sept. 1986	£1·50 (*No.* 1026e)	8·00	☐
15 Sept. 1987	£1·60 (*No.* 1026f)	8·00	☐
23 Aug. 1988	14p, 19p, 20p, 23p, 27p, 28p, 32p, 35p (*Nos.* X903, X954, X957, X963, X968, X970, X975, X978)	5·00	☐
26 Sept. 1989	15p, 20p, 24p, 29p, 30p, 34p, 37p (*Nos.* X905, X958, X965, X972/3, X957, X979)	3·75	☐
4 Sept. 1990	10p, 17p, 22p, 26p, 27p, 31p, 33p (*Nos.* X938a, X909m, X961b, X967b, X968n, X974b, X975a)	3·25	☐

For 1989 and 1990 "1st" and "2nd" and 1990 150th Anniversary of the Penny Black first day covers see pages 86/7 and 90.

Keep this Catalogue up to date month by month with —

The only magazine with the Stanley Gibbons Catalogue supplement – and much more besides!

Please send for a FREE COPY and subscription details to:

Hugh Jefferies
Stanley Gibbons Publications Ltd.,
5 Parkside, Christchurch Road,
Ringwood, Hampshire BH24 3SH
Telephone 0425 472363

370 'A Mountain Road'
(T. P. Flanagan)

371 'Deer's Meadow'
(Tom Carr)

372 'Slieve na brock'
(Colin Middleton)

'Ulster '71' Paintings

1971 (16 JUNE) *Two phosphor bands*

881	**370**	3p multicoloured ..	10	10	☐	☐
882	**371**	7½p multicoloured ..	75	80	☐	☐
883	**372**	9p multicoloured ..	75	80	☐	☐
	Set of 3	.. .. ..	1·40	1·50	☐	☐
	First Day Cover	.. ..		1·75		☐
	Presentation Pack	.. ..	3·00			☐

373 John Keats
(150th Death Anniv)

374 Thomas Gray
(Death Bicentenary)

375 Sir Walter Scott
(Birth Bicentenary)

Literary Anniversaries. Events described above

1971 (28 JULY) *Two phosphor bands*

884	**373**	3p black, gold & bl ..	10	10	☐	☐
885	**374**	5p blk, gold & olive	75	80	☐	☐
886	**375**	7½p black, gold & brn	75	80	☐	☐
	Set of 3	.. .. ..	1·40	1·50	☐	☐
	First Day Cover	.. ..		1·60		☐
	Presentation Pack	.. ..	2·75			☐

376 Servicemen and Nurse
of 1921

377 Roman Centurion

378 Rugby Football, 1871

British Anniversaries. Events described on stamps

1971 (25 AUG.) *Two phosphor bands*

887	**376**	3p multicoloured ..	10	10	☐	☐
888	**377**	7½p multicoloured ..	90	90	☐	☐
889	**378**	9p multicoloured ..	1·00	1·00	☐	☐
	Set of 3	.. .. ..	1·75	1·75	☐	☐
	First Day Cover	.. ..		2·00		☐
	Presentation Pack	.. ..	3·00			☐

379 Physical Sciences Building,
University College of
Wales, Aberystwyth

380 Faraday Building,
Southampton
University

381 Engineering Department,
Leicester University

382 Hexagon Restaurant,
Essex University

British Architecture (Modern University Buildings)

1971 (22 Sept.) *Two phosphor bands*

890	**379**	3p multicoloured ..	10	10	☐	☐
891	**380**	5p multicoloured ..	20	25	☐	☐
892	**381**	7½p ochre, black and purple-brown. ..	80	80	☐	☐
893	**382**	9p multicoloured ..	1·60	1·60	☐	☐
		Set of 4	2·50	2·50	☐	☐
		First Day Cover		2·50		☐
		Presentation Pack	3·50		☐	

Collectors Pack 1971

1971 (29 Sept.) *Comprises Nos.* 835/40 *and* 881/93

	Collectors Pack	32·00	☐

383 'Dream of the Wise Men'

384 'Adoration of the Magi'

385 'Ride of the Magi'

Christmas

1971 (13 Oct.) *Two phosphor bands* (3p, 7½p) *or one centre phosphor band* (2½p)

894	**383**	2½p multicoloured ..	10	10	☐	☐
895	**384**	3p multicoloured ..	10	10	☐	☐
896	**385**	7½p multicoloured ..	90	1·00	☐	☐
		Set of 3	1·00	1·10	☐	☐
		First Day Cover		1·75		☐
		Presentation Pack	3·25		☐	

386 Sir James Clark Ross

387 Sir Martin Frobisher

388 Henry Hudson

389 Capt. Robert F. Scott

British Polar Explorers

1972 (16 Feb.) *Two phosphor bands*

897	**386**	3p multicoloured ..	10	10	☐	☐
898	**387**	5p multicoloured ..	20	20	☐	☐
899	**388**	7½p multicoloured ..	65	65	☐	☐
900	**389**	9p multicoloured ..	1·10	1·10	☐	☐
		Set of 4	1·75	1·75	☐	☐
		First Day Cover		2·00		☐
		Presentation Pack	3·25		☐	

390 Statuette of Tutankhamun

391 19th-century Coastguard

392 Ralph Vaughan Williams and Score

Anniversaries. Events described on stamps

1972 (26 Apr.) *Two phosphor bands*

901	**390**	3p multicoloured ..	10	10	☐	☐
902	**391**	7½p multicoloured ..	70	80	☐	☐
903	**392**	9p multicoloured ..	70	65	☐	☐
		Set of 3	1·25	1·40	☐	☐
		First Day Cover		1·90		☐
		Presentation Pack	3·25		☐	

393 St Andrew's, Greensted-juxta-Ongar, Essex

394 All Saints, Earls Barton, Northants

395 St Andrew's, Letheringsett, Norfolk

396 St Andrew's, Helpringham, Lincs

397 St Mary the Virgin, Huish Episcopi, Somerset

British Architecture (Village Churches)

1972 (21 JUNE) *Two phosphor bands*

904	**393**	3p multicoloured ..	10	10	☐	☐
905	**394**	4p multicoloured ..	20	20	☐	☐
906	**395**	5p multicoloured ..	20	25	☐	☐
907	**396**	7½p multicoloured ..	1·40	1·50	☐	☐
908	**397**	9p multicoloured ..	1·60	1·75	☐	☐
		Set of 5	3·25	3·50	☐	☐
		First Day Cover		3·50		☐
		Presentation Pack ..	5·00		☐	

'Belgica '72' Souvenir Pack

1972 (24 JUNE) *Comprises Nos. 894/6 and 904/8*

Souvenir Pack .. .. .. 15·00   ☐

398 Microphones, 1924–69

399 Horn Loudspeaker

400 TV Camera, 1972

401 Oscillator and Spark Transmitter, 1897

Broadcasting Anniversaries. Events described on stamps

1972 (13 SEPT.) *Two phosphor bands*

909	**398**	3p multicoloured ..	10	10	☐	☐
910	**399**	5p multicoloured ..	15	20	☐	☐
911	**400**	7½p multicoloured ..	1·00	1·00	☐	☐
912	**401**	9p multicoloured ..	1·00	1·00	☐	☐
		Set of 4	2·00	2·00	☐	☐
		First Day Cover		2·00		☐
		Presentation Pack	3·25		☐	

402 Angel holding Trumpet

403 Angel playing Lute

404 Angel playing Harp

Christmas

1972 (18 Oct.) *Two phosphor bands (3p, 7½p) or one centre phosphor band (2½p)*

913	**402**	2½p multicoloured ..	10	15	☐	☐
914	**403**	3p multicoloured ..	10	15	☐	☐
915	**404**	7½p multicoloured ..	70	60	☐	☐
		Set of 3	75	80	☐	☐
		First Day Cover		1·40		☐
		Presentation Pack	2·25			☐

Oak Quercus robur   **407** Oak Tree

British Trees (1st issue)

1973 (28 Feb.) *Two phosphor bands*

922	**407**	9p multicoloured ..	50	45	☐	☐
		First Day Cover		1·00		☐
		Presentation Pack	2·50			☐

See also No. 949.

405 Queen Elizabeth II and Prince Philip

406 'Europe'

Royal Silver Wedding

1972 (20 Nov.) *3p 'all-over' phosphor, 20p without phosphor*

916	**405**	3p brownish black, deep blue and silver	20	20	☐	☐
917		20p brownish black, reddish purple and silver ..	80	80	☐	☐
		Set of 2	1·00	1·00	☐	☐
		First Day Cover		1·25		☐
		Presentation Pack	2·00			☐
		Presentation Pack (Japanese)	4·00			☐
		Souvenir Book	3·00			☐
		Gutter Pair (3p)	90			☐
		Traffic Light Gutter Pair (3p)	22·00			☐

Collectors Pack 1972

1972 (20 Nov.) *Comprises Nos. 897/917*

	Collectors Pack	35·00		☐

Nos. 920/1 were issued horizontally *se-tenant* throughout the sheet.

Britain's Entry into European Communities

1973 (3 Jan.) *Two phosphor bands*

919	**406**	3p multicoloured ..	10	10	☐	☐
920		5p multicoloured (blue jigsaw) ..	25	35	☐	☐
		a. Pair. Nos. 920/1	1·50	1·60	☐	☐
921		5p multicoloured (green jigsaw)	25	35	☐	☐
		Set of 3	1·50	70	☐	☐
		First Day Cover		1·60		☐
		Presentation Pack	2·50			☐

408 David Livingstone

409 H. M. Stanley

The above were issued horizontally *se-tenant* throughout the sheet.

410 Sir Francis Drake

411 Sir Walter Raleigh

412 Charles Sturt

41

British Explorers

1973 (18 APR.) 'All-over' phosphor

923	**408**	3p multicoloured ..	25	20	☐	☐
		a. Pair. Nos. 923/4	1·60	1·60	☐	☐
924	**409**	3p multicoloured ..	25	20	☐	☐
925	**410**	5p multicoloured ..	30	30	☐	☐
926	**411**	7½p multicoloured ..	35	30	☐	☐
927	**412**	9p multicoloured ..	40	40	☐	☐
		Set of 5	2·50	1·25	☐	☐
		First Day Cover		2·50		☐
		Presentation Pack	4·00			☐

413   **414**

415

County Cricket 1873–1973

1973 (16 MAY) *Designs show sketches of W. G. Grace by Harry Furniss. Queen's head in gold.* 'All-over' phosphor

928	**413**	3p black and brown	10	10	☐	☐
929	**414**	7½p black and green	1·25	1·40	☐	☐
930	**415**	9p black and blue	1·40	1·40	☐	☐
		Set of 3	2·40	2·50	☐	☐
		First Day Cover		2·50		☐
		Presentation Pack	3·50			☐
		Souvenir Book	7·50			☐
		PHQ Card (No. 928)	50·00	£140	☐	☐

For full information on all future British issues, collectors should write to the British Post Office Philatelic Bureau, 20 Brandon Street, Edinburgh EH3 5TT

416 'Self-portrait' (Sir Joshua Reynolds)

417 'Self-portrait' (Sir Henry Raeburn)

418 'Nelly O'Brien' (Sir Joshua Reynolds)

419 'Rev R. Walker (The Skater)' (Sir Henry Raeburn)

Artistic Anniversaries. Events described on stamps

1973 (4 JULY) 'All-over' phosphor

931	**416**	3p multicoloured ..	10	10	☐	☐
932	**417**	5p multicoloured ..	20	25	☐	☐
933	**418**	7½p multicoloured ..	70	70	☐	☐
934	**419**	9p multicoloured ..	90	90	☐	☐
		Set of 4	1·60	1·75	☐	☐
		First Day Cover		1·90		☐
		Presentation Pack	2·40			☐

420 Court Masque Costumes   **421** St Paul's Church, Covent Garden

422 Prince's Lodging, Newmarket   **423** Court Masque Stage Scene

The 3p and 5p values were printed horizontally *se-tenant* within the sheet.

400th Anniversary of the Birth of Inigo Jones

1973 (15 Aug.) *'All-over' phosphor*

935	**420**	3p deep mauve, black and gold ..	10	15	☐	☐
		a. Pair. Nos. 935/6	35	40	☐	☐
936	**421**	3p deep brown, black and gold ..	10	15	☐	☐
937	**422**	5p blue, black and gold ..	40	45	☐	☐
		a. Pair. Nos. 937/8	2·40	2·40	☐	☐
938	**423**	5p grey-olive, black and gold	40	45	☐	☐
		Set of 4	2·50	1·10	☐	☐
		First Day Cover		2·00		☐
		Presentation Pack	2·75		☐	
		PHQ Card (No. 936)	£140	70·00	☐	☐

424 Palace of Westminster seen from Whitehall

425 Palace of Westminster seen from Millbank

19th Commonwealth Parliamentary Conference

1973 (12 Sept.) *'All-over' phosphor*

939	**424**	8p black, grey and pale buff	50	60	☐	☐
940	**425**	10p gold and black ..	50	40	☐	☐
		Set of 2	1·00	1·00	☐	☐
		First Day Cover		1·25		☐
		Presentation Pack	2·00		☐	
		Souvenir Book	8·00		☐	
		PHQ Card (No. 939) ..	48·00	90·00	☐	☐

426 Princess Anne and Captain Mark Phillips

Royal Wedding

1973 (14 Nov.) *'All-over' phosphor*

941	**426**	3½p violet and silver	10	10	☐	☐
942		20p brown and silver	90	1·00	☐	☐
		Set of 2	1·00	1·10	☐	☐
		First Day Cover		1·25		☐
		Presentation Pack	2·00		☐	
		PHQ Card (No. 941)	10·00	22·00	☐	☐
		Set of 2 Gutter Pairs ..	6·00		☐	
		Set of 2 Traffic Light Gutter Pairs	90·00		☐	

427

428

429

430

431

432 'Good King Wenceslas, the Page and Peasant'

The 3p values depict the carol 'Good King Wenceslas' and were printed horizontally *se-tenant* within the sheet.

Christmas

1973 (28 Nov.) *One phosphor band (3p) or 'all-over' phosphor (3½p)*

943	**427**	3p multicoloured ..	15	15	☐	☐
		a. Strip of 5. Nos. 943/7 ..	3·00	2·75	☐	☐
944	**428**	3p multicoloured ..	15	15	☐	☐
945	**429**	3p multicoloured ..	15	15	☐	☐
946	**430**	3p multicoloured ..	15	15	☐	☐
947	**431**	3p multicoloured ..	15	15	☐	☐
948	**432**	3½p multicoloured ..	15	15	☐	☐
		Set of 6	3·00	80	☐	☐
		First Day Cover		2·75		☐
		Presentation Pack	3·25		☐	

Collectors Pack 1973

1973 (28 Nov.) *Comprises Nos.* 919/48

	Collectors Pack	28·00		☐

433 Horse Chestnut

43

British Trees (2nd issue)

1974 (27 FEB.) *'All-over' phosphor*

949	**433**	10p multicoloured ..	50	50	☐	☐
		First Day Cover		1·00		☐
		Presentation Pack	2·25		☐	
		PHQ Card	£125	70·00	☐	☐
		Gutter Pair	3·00		☐	
		Traffic Light Gutter Pair ..	50·00		☐	

434 First Motor Fire-engine, 1904

435 Prize-winning Fire-engine, 1863

436 Steam Fire-engine, 1830

437 Fire-engine, 1766

200th Anniversary of Public Fire Services

1974 (24 APR.) *'All-over' phosphor*

950	**434**	3½p multicoloured ..	10	10	☐	☐
951	**435**	5½p multicoloured ..	25	25	☐	☐
952	**436**	8p multicoloured ..	60	65	☐	☐
953	**437**	10p multicoloured ..	80	85	☐	☐
		Set of 4	1·50	1·60	☐	☐
		First Day Cover		3·00		☐
		Presentation Pack	2·00		☐	
		PHQ Card (No. 950) ..	£125	60·00	☐	☐
		Set of 4 Gutter Pairs ..	4·00		☐	
		Set of 4 Traffic Light Gutter Pairs	50·00		☐	

438 P & O Packet Peninsular, 1888

439 Farman Biplane, 1911

440 Airmail-blue Van and Postbox, 1930

441 Imperial Airways 'C' Class Flying-boat, 1937

Centenary of Universal Postal Union

1974 (12 JUNE) *'All-over' phosphor*

954	**438**	3½p multicoloured ..	10	10	☐	☐
955	**439**	5½p multicoloured ..	20	25	☐	☐
956	**440**	8p multicoloured ..	30	35	☐	☐
957	**441**	10p multicoloured ..	50	40	☐	☐
		Set of 4	1·00	1·00	☐	☐
		First Day Cover		1·40		☐
		Presentation Pack	2·00		☐	
		Set of 4 Gutter Pairs ..	4·00		☐	
		Set of 4 Traffic Light Gutter Pairs	40·00		☐	

442 Robert the Bruce

443 Owain Glyndŵr

444 Henry the Fifth

445 The Black Prince

Medieval Warriors

1974 (10 JULY) *'All-over' phosphor*

958	**442**	4½p multicoloured ..	10	10	☐	☐
959	**443**	5½p multicoloured ..	20	25	☐	☐
960	**444**	8p multicoloured ..	85	90	☐	☐
961	**445**	10p multicoloured ..	85	90	☐	☐
		Set of 4	1·90	1·90	☐	☐
		First Day Cover		2·50		☐
		Presentation Pack.. ..	3·50		☐	
		PHQ Cards (set of 4) ..	36·00	26·00	☐	☐
		Set of 4 Gutter Pairs ..	6·00		☐	
		Set of 4 Traffic Light Gutter Pairs	70·00		☐	

446 Churchill in Royal Yacht Squadron Uniform

447 Prime Minister, 1940

448 Secretary for War and Air, 1919

449 War Correspondent, South Africa, 1899

Birth Centenary of Sir Winston Churchill

1974 (9 OCT.) *Queen's head and inscription in silver. 'All-over' phosphor*

962	**446**	4½p green and blue	15	15	□	□
963	**447**	5½p grey and black	20	25	□	□
964	**448**	8p rose and lake ..	45	40	□	□
965	**449**	10p stone and brown	45	45	□	□
	Set of 4		1·10	1·10	□	□
	First Day Cover ..			1·60		□
	Presentation Pack ..		1·50		□	
	Souvenir Book		2·50		□	
	PHQ Card (No. 963)		8·00	12·00	□	□
	Set of 4 Gutter Pairs ..		4·00		□	
	Set of 4 Traffic Light					
	Gutter Pairs ..		40·00		□	

450 'Adoration of the Magi' (York Minster, *c.* 1355)

451 'The Nativity' (St Helen's Church, Norwich, *c.* 1480)

452 'Virgin and Child' (Ottery St Mary Church, *c.* 1350)

453 'Virgin and Child' (Worcester Cathedral, *c.* 1224)

Christmas

1974 (27 NOV.) *Designs show church roof bosses. One phosphor band (3½p) or 'all-over' phosphor (others)*

966	**450**	3½p multicoloured ..	10	10	□	□
967	**451**	4½p multicoloured ..	10	10	□	□
968	**452**	8p multicoloured ..	45	45	□	□
969	**453**	10p multicoloured ..	50	50	□	□
	Set of 4		1·00	1·00	□	□
	First Day Cover ..			1·40		□
	Presentation Pack ..		1·50		□	
	Set of 4 Gutter Pairs ..		4·00		□	
	Set of 4 Traffic Light					
	Gutter Pairs		50·00		□	

Collectors Pack 1974

1974 (27 NOV.) *Comprises Nos.* 949/69

Collectors Pack	10·00		□

454 Invalid in Wheelchair

Health and Handicap Funds

1975 (22 JAN.) *'All-over' phosphor*

970	**454**	4½p + 1½p azure and blue	25	25	□	□
	First Day Cover			65		□
	Gutter Pair		50		□	
	Traffic Light Gutter Pair		80		□	

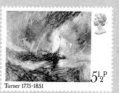

455 'Peace – Burial at Sea'

456 'Snowstorm – Steamer off a Harbour's Mouth'

457 'The Arsenal, Venice'

458 'St Laurent'

Birth Bicentenary of J. M. W. Turner

1975 (19 FEB.) *'All-over' phosphor*

971	**455**	4½p multicoloured ..	10	10	□	□
972	**456**	5½p multicoloured ..	15	15	□	□
973	**457**	8p multicoloured ..	40	40	□	□
974	**458**	10p multicoloured ..	45	45	□	□
	Set of 4		1·00	1·00	□	□
	First Day Cover			1·25		□
	Presentation Pack		2·00		□	
	PHQ Card (No. 972)		30·00	11·00	□	□
	Set of 4 Gutter Pairs ..		2·00		□	
	Set of 4 Traffic Light					
	Gutter Pairs		6·00		□	

459 Charlotte Square, Edinburgh

460 The Rows, Chester

The above were printed horizontally *se-tenant* throughout the sheet.

461 Royal Observatory, Greenwich

462 St George's Chapel, Windsor

463 National Theatre, London

European Architectural Heritage Year

1975 (23 APR.) *'All-over' phosphor*

975	**459**	7p multicoloured ..	30	20	☐	☐
		a. Pair. Nos. 975/6	75	.70	☐	☐
976	**460**	7p multicoloured ..	30	20	☐	☐
977	**461**	8p multicoloured ..	20	25	☐	☐
978	**462**	10p multicoloured ..	25	25	☐	☐
979	**463**	12p multicoloured ..	30	35	☐	☐
	Set of 5		1·25	1·10	☐	☐
	First Day Cover			2·00		☐
	Presentation Pack ..		2·00		☐	
	PHQ Cards (Nos. 975/7) ..		7·00	10·00	☐	☐
	Set of 5 Gutter Pairs ..		4·00		☐	
	Set of 5 Traffic Light					
	Gutter Pairs		15·00		☐	

464 Sailing Dinghies

465 Racing Keel Boats

466 Cruising Yachts

467 Multihulls

Sailing

1975 (11 JUNE) *'All-over' phosphor*

980	**464**	7p multicoloured ..	20	20	☐	☐
981	**465**	8p multicoloured ..	20	20	☐	☐
982	**466**	10p multicoloured ..	25	25	☐	☐
983	**467**	12p multicoloured ..	45	45	☐	☐
	Set of 4		1·00	1·00	☐	☐
	First Day Cover			1·75		☐
	Presentation Pack		1·25		☐	
	PHQ Card (No. 981)		5·00	9·00	☐	☐
	Set of 4 Gutter Pairs ..		2·00		☐	
	Set of 4 Traffic Light					
	Gutter Pairs		20·00		☐	

468 Stephenson's Locomotion, 1825

469 Abbotsford, 1876

470 Caerphilly Castle, 1923

471 High Speed Train, 1975

150th Anniversary of Public Railways

1975 (13 AUG.) *'All-over' phosphor*

984	**468**	7p multicoloured ..	30	35	☐	☐
985	**469**	8p multicoloured ..	30	40	☐	☐
986	**470**	10p multicoloured ..	40	45	☐	☐
987	**471**	12p multicoloured ..	50	60	☐	☐
	Set of 4		1·40	1·60	☐	☐
	First Day Cover			2·50		☐
	Presentation Pack		2·25		☐	
	Souvenir Book		3·00		☐	
	PHQ Cards (set of 4) ..		60·00	25·00	☐	☐
	Set of 4 Gutter Pairs ..		3·00		☐	
	Set of 4 Traffic Light					
	Gutter Pairs		12·00		☐	

472 Palace of Westminster

62nd Inter-Parliamentary Union Conference

1975 (3 SEPT.) *'All-over' phosphor*

988	**472**	12p multicoloured ..	50	50	☐	☐
		First Day Cover		1·00		☐
		Presentation Pack	1·25		☐	
		Gutter Pair	1·00		☐	
		Traffic Light Gutter Pair	3·00		☐	

473 'Emma and Mr Woodhouse' (*Emma*)

474 'Catherine Morland' (*Northanger Abbey*)

475 'Mr Darcy' (*Pride and Prejudice*)

476 'Mary and Henry Crawford' (*Mansfield Park*)

Birth Bicentenary of Jane Austen (Novelist)

1975 (22 OCT.) *'All-over' phosphor*

989	**473**	8½p multicoloured ..	20	20	☐	☐
990	**474**	10p multicoloured ..	25	25	☐	☐
991	**475**	11p multicoloured ..	40	45	☐	☐
992	**476**	13p multicoloured ..	40	40	☐	☐
		Set of 4	1·10	1·10	☐	☐
		First Day Cover		1·40		☐
		Presentation Pack	2·00		☐	
		PHQ Cards (set of 4) ..	16·00	15·00	☐	☐
		Set of 4 Gutter Pairs ..	2·25		☐	
		Set of 4 Traffic Light Gutter Pairs	8·00		☐	

477 Angels with Harp and Lute

478 Angel with Mandolin

479 Angel with Horn

480 Angel with Trumpet

Christmas

1975 (26 NOV.) *One phosphor band* (6½p), *phosphor-inked* (8½p) *(background) or 'all-over' phosphor (others)*

993	**477**	6½p multicoloured ..	20	15	☐	☐
994	**478**	8½p multicoloured ..	20	20	☐	☐
995	**479**	11p multicoloured ..	40	50	☐	☐
996	**480**	13p multicoloured ..	40	45	☐	☐
		Set of 4	1·10	1·10	☐	☐
		First Day Cover		1·25		☐
		Presentation Pack	2·00		☐	
		Set of 4 Gutter Pairs ..	2·25		☐	
		Set of 4 Traffic Light Gutter Pairs	8·00		☐	

Collectors Pack 1975

1975 (26 NOV.) *Comprises Nos.* 970/96

	Collectors Pack	8·00	☐

481 Housewife

482 Policeman

483 District Nurse

484 Industrialist

Telephone Centenary

1976 (10 Mar.) *'All-over' phosphor*

997	**481**	8½p multicoloured ..	20	20	☐	☐
998	**482**	10p multicoloured ..	25	25	☐	☐
999	**483**	11p multicoloured ..	40	45	☐	☐
1000	**484**	13p multicoloured ..	40	45	☐	☐
		Set of 4	1·10	1·10	☐	☐
		First Day Cover		1·25		☐
		Presentation Pack ..	2·00		☐	
		Set of 4 Gutter Pairs ..	2·25		☐	
		Set of 4 Traffic Light Gutter Pairs	8·00		☐	

485 Hewing Coal (Thomas Hepburn)
486 Machinery (Robert Owen)

487 Chimney Cleaning (Lord Shaftesbury)
488 Hands clutching Prison Bars (Elizabeth Fry)

Social Reformers

1976 (28 Apr.) *'All-over phosphor*

1001	**485**	8½p multicoloured ..	20	20	☐	☐
1002	**486**	10p multicoloured ..	25	25	☐	☐
1003	**487**	11p black, slate-grey and drab ..	40	45	☐	☐
1004	**488**	13p slate-grey, black and green	40	45	☐	☐
		Set of 4	1·10	1·10	☐	☐
		First Day Cover ..		1·25		☐
		Presentation Pack ..	2·00		☐	
		PHQ Card (No. 1001) ..	5·00	7·00	☐	☐
		Set of 4 Gutter Pairs ..	2·25		☐	
		Set of 4 Traffic Light Gutter Pairs	8·00		☐	

489 Benjamin Franklin (bust by Jean-Jacques Caffieri)

Bicentenary of American Independence

1976 (2 June) *'All-over' phosphor*

1005	**489**	11p multicoloured ..	50	50	☐	☐
		First Day Cover		60		☐
		Presentation Pack ..	1·00		☐	
		PHQ Card	4·00	8·50	☐	
		Gutter Pair	1·00		☐	
		Traffic Light Gutter Pair ..	2·00		☐	

490 'Elizabeth of Glamis'
491 'Grandpa Dickson'

492 'Rosa Mundi'
493 'Sweet Briar'

Centenary of Royal National Rose Society

1976 (30 June) *'All-over' phosphor*

1006	**490**	8½p multicoloured ..	20	20	☐	☐
1007	**491**	10p multicoloured ..	30	30	☐	☐
1008	**492**	11p multicoloured ..	35	40	☐	☐
1009	**493**	13p multicoloured ..	35	35	☐	☐
		Set of 4	1·10	1·10	☐	☐
		First Day Cover ..		1·75		☐
		Presentation Pack ..	2·10		☐	
		PHQ Cards (set of 4) ..	30·00	14·00	☐	☐
		Set of 4 Gutter Pairs	2·40		☐	
		Set of 4 Traffic Light Gutter Pairs	10·00		☐	

494 Archdruid
495 Morris Dancing

496 Scots Piper

497 Welsh Harpist

British Cultural Traditions

1976 (4 AUG.) 'All-over' phosphor

1010	**494**	8½p multicoloured ..	20	20	☐	☐
1011	**495**	10p multicoloured ..	30	30	☐	☐
1012	**496**	11p multicoloured ..	35	35	☐	☐
1013	**497**	13p multicoloured ..	35	35	☐	☐
		Set of 4	1·10	1·10	☐	☐
		First Day Cover		1·25		☐
		Presentation Pack ..	2·00		☐	
		PHQ Cards (set of 4)	14·00	8·50	☐	☐
		Set of 4 Gutter Pairs ..	2·25		☐	
		Set of 4 Traffic Light Gutter Pairs	9·00		☐	

498 The Canterbury Tales

499 The Tretyse of Love

500 Game and Playe of Chesse

501 Early Printing Press

500th Anniversary of British Printing

1976 (29 SEPT.) 'All-over' phosphor

1014	**498**	8½p blk, bl & gold	20	20	☐	☐
1015	**499**	10p blk, olive-grn & gold	25	30	☐	☐
1016	**500**	11p blk, grey & gold ..	35	40	☐	☐
1017	**501**	13p brn, ochre & gold ..	40	45	☐	☐
		Set of 4	1·10	1·10	☐	☐
		First Day Cover		1·25		☐
		Presentation Pack	2·10		☐	
		PHQ Cards (set of 4) ..	10·00	8·50	☐	☐
		Set of 4 Gutter Pairs	2·25		☐	
		Set of 4 Traffic Light Gutter Pairs	7·00		☐	

502 Virgin and Child

503 Angel with Crown

504 Angel appearing to Shepherds

505 The Three Kings

Christmas

1976 (24 Nov.) Designs show English mediaeval embroidery. One phosphor band (6½p) or 'all-over' phosphor (others)

1018	**502**	6½p multicoloured ..	15	15	☐	☐
1019	**503**	8½p multicoloured ..	20	20	☐	☐
1020	**504**	11p multicoloured ..	35	40	☐	☐
1021	**505**	13p multicoloured ..	40	40	☐	☐
		Set of 4	1·00	1·10	☐	☐
		First Day Cover		1·25		☐
		Presentation Pack ..	2·00		☐	
		PHQ Cards (set of 4)	3·00	7·00	☐	☐
		Set of 4 Gutter Pairs	2·00		☐	
		Set of 4 Traffic Light Gutter Pairs	7·00		☐	

Collectors Pack 1976

1976 (24 Nov.) Comprises Nos. 997/1021

Collectors Pack	12·00		☐

506 Lawn Tennis

507 Table Tennis

508 Squash

509 Badminton

Racket Sports

1977 (12 Jan.) *Phosphorised paper*

1022	**506**	8½p multicoloured ..	20	20	☐	☐
1023	**507**	10p multicoloured ..	30	30	☐	☐
1024	**508**	11p multicoloured ..	35	40	☐	☐
1025	**509**	13p multicoloured ..	40	40	☐	☐
		Set of 4	1·10	1·10	☐	☐
		First Day Cover ..		1·50		☐
		Presentation Pack ..	2·00		☐	
		PHQ Cards (set of 4)	6·00	8·50	☐	☐
		Set of 4 Gutter Pairs ..	2·25		☐	
		Set of 4 Traffic Light Gutter Pairs	7·00		☐	

510

1977 (2 Feb.)–**87** *Type 510 Ordinary paper*

1026		£1 green and olive	2·50	20	☐	☐
1026*b*		£1·30 drab & dp grnish bl	10·00	7·50	☐	☐
1026*c*		£1·33 pale mve & grey-blk ..	8·50	6·00	☐	☐
1026*d*		£1·41 drab & dp grnish bl	9·00	5·00	☐	☐
1026*e*		£1·50 pale mve & grey-blk ..	4·50	3·00	☐	☐
1026*f*		£1·60 drab and dp grnish bl	4·50	2·75	☐	☐
1027		£2 green and brown ..	5·00	75	☐	☐
1028		£5 pink and blue	12·00	3·50	☐	☐
		Presentation Pack (Nos. 1026, 1027/8)	17·00		☐	
		Presentation Pack (No. 1026*f*)	2·75		☐	

For First Day Cover prices see page 36.

511 Steroids – Conformational Analysis

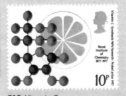

512 Vitamin C – Synthesis

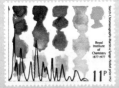

513 Starch – Chromatography

514 Salt – Crystallography

Centenary of Royal Institute of Chemistry

1977 (2 Mar.) *'All-over' phosphor*

1029	**511**	8½p multicoloured ..	20	20	☐	☐
1030	**512**	10p multicoloured ..	30	30	☐	☐
1031	**513**	11p multicoloured ..	35	35	☐	☐
1032	.**514**	13p multicoloured ..	40	40	☐	☐
		Set of 4	1·10	1·10	☐	☐
		First Day Cover ..		1·40		☐
		Presentation Pack ..	2·40		☐	
		PHQ Cards (set of 4)	6·00	9·00	☐	☐
		Set of 4 Gutter Pairs ..	2·25		☐	
		Set of 4 Traffic Light Gutter Pairs	7·00		☐	

515

516

517

518

(The designs differ in the decorations of 'ER'.)

Silver Jubilee

1977 (11 May–15 June) *'All-over' phosphor*

1033	**515**	8½p multicoloured ..	20	20	☐	☐
1034		9p mult (15 June) ..	25	25	☐	☐
1035	**516**	10p multicoloured ..	25	30	☐	☐
1036	**517**	11p multicoloured ..	30	35	☐	☐
1037	**518**	13p multicoloured ..	40	40	☐	☐
		Set of 5	1·25	1·40	☐	☐
		First Day Covers (2)		1·75		☐
		Presentation Pack (ex 9p)	1·75		☐	
		Souvenir Book (ex 9p) ..	4·00		☐	
		PHQ Cards (set of 5) ..	10·00	8·00	☐	☐
		Set of 5 Gutter Pairs ..	2·75		☐	
		Set of 5 Traffic Light Gutter Pairs	3·75		☐	

519 'Gathering of Nations'

Commonwealth Heads of Government Meeting, London

1977 (8 June) *'All-over' phosphor*

1038	519	13p	black, deep green rose and silver	50	50	□	□
		First Day Cover	.. .. ..		1·00		□
		Presentation Pack	.. ..	1·00		□	
		PHQ Card	.. .. ..	2·50	3·75	□	□
		Gutter Pair	.. .. ..	1·00		□	
		Traffic Light Gutter Pair	..	1·25		□	

520 Hedgehog

521 Brown Hare

522 Red Squirrel

523 Otter

T **520/4** were printed together, *se-tenant*, throughout the sheet

524 Badger

British Wildlife

1977 (5 Oct.) *'All-over' phosphor*

1039	520	9p	multicoloured ..	25	20	□	□
		a. Strip of 5. Nos. 1039/43 ..		1·75	1·75	□	□
1040	521	9p	multicoloured ..	25	20	□	□
1041	522	9p	multicoloured ..	25	20	□	□
1042	523	9p	multicoloured ..	25	20	□	□
1043	524	9p	multicoloured ..	25	20	□	□
		Set of 5	.. ..	1·75	90	□	□
		First Day Cover	.. ..		2·25		□
		Presentation Pack	.. ..	2·10		□	
		PHQ Cards (set of 5) ..		4·00	4·25	□	□
		Gutter Strip of 10	..	3·75		□	
		Traffic Light Gutter Strip of 10		4·00		□	

525 'Three French Hens, Two Turtle Doves and a Partridge in a Pear Tree'

526 'Six Geese a-laying, Five Gold Rings, Four Colly Birds'

527 'Eight Maids a-milking, Seven Swans a-swimming'

528 'Ten Pipers piping, Nine Drummers drumming'

529 'Twelve Lords a-leaping, Eleven Ladies dancing'

530 A Partridge in a Pear Tree'

T **525/30** depict the carol 'The Twelve Days of Christmas'. T **525/29** were printed horizontally *se-tenant* throughout the sheet.

Christmas

1977 (23 Nov.) *One centre phosphor band (7p) or 'all-over' phosphor (9p)*

1044	525	7p	multicoloured ..	15	15	□	□
		a. Strip of 5 Nos. 1044/8 ..		1·00	1·10	□	□
1045	526	7p	multicoloured ..	15	15	□	□
1046	527	7p	multicoloured ..	15	15	□	□
1047	528	7p	multicoloured ..	15	15	□	□
1048	529	7p	multicoloured ..	15	15	□	□
1049	530	9p	multicoloured ..	20	20	□	□
		Set of 6	.. ..	1·10	85	□	□
		First Day Cover	.. ..		1·40		□
		Presentation Pack	.. ..	2·00		□	
		PHQ Cards (set of 6)	..	2·50	4·00	□	□
		Set of 6 Gutter Pairs	..	2·50		□	
		Set of 6 Traffic Light Gutter Pairs		4·00		□	

Collectors Pack 1977

1977 (23 Nov.) *Comprises Nos.* 1022/5, 1029/49

	Collectors Pack	..	7·00	□

531 Oil—North Sea
Production Platform

532 Coal—Modern
Pithead

533 Natural Gas—Flame
Rising from Sea

534 Electricity—Nuclear Power
Station and Uranium Atom

Energy Resources

1978 (25 Jan.) *'All-over' phosphor*

1050	**531**	9p multicoloured ..	25	20	☐	☐
1051	**532**	10½p multicoloured ..	25	35	☐	☐
1052	**533**	11p multicoloured ..	35	40	☐	☐
1053	**534**	13p multicoloured ..	40	40	☐	☐
		Set of 4	1·10	1·10	☐	☐
		First Day Cover		1·25		☐
		Presentation Pack ..	2·00		☐	
		PHQ Cards (set of 4) ..	2·50	4·00	☐	☐
		Set of 4 Gutter Pairs ..	2·25		☐	
		Set of 4 Traffic Light				
		Gutter Pairs	4·00		☐	

535 Tower of London

536 Holyroodhouse

537 Caernarvon Castle

538 Hampton Court Palace

British Architecture (Historic Buildings)

1978 (1 Mar.) *'All-over' phosphor*

1054	**535**	9p multicoloured ..	25	20	☐	☐
1055	**536**	10½p. multicoloured ..	25	30	☐	☐
1056	**537**	11p multicoloured ..	35	35	☐	☐
1057	**538**	13p multicoloured ..	40	40	☐	☐
		Set of 4	1·10	1·10	☐	☐
		First Day Cover		1·25		☐
		Presentation Pack	2·00		☐	
		PHQ Cards (set of 4)	2·50	3·50	☐	☐
		Set of 4 Gutter Pairs ..	2·25		☐	
		Set of 4 Traffic Light				
		Gutter Pairs	4·00		☐	
MS1058	121×90 mm. Nos. 1054/57		1·50	1·60	☐	☐
		First Day Cover		2·00		☐

No. **MS**1058 was sold at 53½p, the premium being used for
the London 1980 Stamp Exhibition.

539 State Coach

540 St Edward's Crown

541 The Sovereign's Orb

542 Imperial State Crown

25th Anniversary of Coronation

1978 (31 May) *'All-over' phosphor*

1059	**539**	9p gold and blue ..	20	20	☐	☐
1060	**540**	10½p gold and red ..	25	30	☐	☐
1061	**541**	11p gold and green ..	35	40	☐	☐
1062	**542**	13p gold and violet ..	40	40	☐	☐
		Set of 4	1·10	1·10	☐	☐
		First Day Cover		1·25		☐
		Presentation Pack	1·50		☐	
		Souvenir Book	4·00		☐	
		PHQ Cards (set of 4)	2·50	2·25	☐	☐
		Set of 4 Gutter Pairs ..	2·25		☐	
		Set of 4 Traffic Light				
		Gutter Pairs	4·00		☐	

543 Shire Horse

544 Shetland Pony

545 Welsh Pony

546 Thoroughbred

Horses

1978 (5 July) *'All-over' phosphor*

1063	**543**	9p multicoloured ..	20	25	☐	☐
1064	**544**	10½p multicoloured ..	25	30	☐	☐
1065	**545**	11p multicoloured ..	35	35	☐	☐
1066	**546**	13p multicoloured ..	40	40	☐	☐
	Set of 4		1·10	1·10	☐	☐
	First Day Cover			1·50		☐
	Presentation Pack		1·50		☐	
	PHQ Cards (set of 4)		2·50	3·50	☐	☐
	Set of 4 Gutter Pairs		2·25		☐	
	Set of 4 Traffic Light Gutter Pairs		4·00		☐	

547 Penny-farthing and 1884 Safety Bicycle

548 1920 Touring Bicycles

549 Modern Small-wheel Bicycles

550 1978 Road-racers

Centenaries of Cyclists Touring Club and British Cycling Federation

1978 (2 Aug.) *'All-over' phosphor*

1067	**547**	9p multicoloured ..	20	20	☐	☐
1068	**548**	10½p multicoloured ..	25	35	☐	☐
1069	**549**	11p multicoloured ..	35	35	☐	☐
1070	**550**	13p multicoloured ..	40	40	☐	☐
	Set of 4		1·10	1·10	☐	☐
	First Day Cover			1·25		☐
	Presentation Pack		1·50		☐	
	PHQ Cards (set of 4)		1·50	2·75	☐	☐
	Set of 4 Gutter Pairs		2·25		☐	
	Set of 4 Traffic Light Gutter Pairs		4·00		☐	

551 Singing Carols round the Christmas Tree

552 The Waits

553 18th-Century Carol Singers

554 'The Boar's Head Carol'

Christmas

1978 (22 Nov.) *One centre posphor band (7p) or 'all-over' phosphor (others)*

1071	**551**	7p multicoloured ..	20	20	☐	☐
1072	**552**	9p multicoloured ..	25	25	☐	☐
1073	**553**	11p multicoloured ..	30	35	☐	☐
1074	**554**	13p multicoloured ..	35	35	☐	☐
	Set of 4		1·00	1·00	☐	☐
	First Day Cover			1·00		☐
	Presentation Pack		1·40		☐	
	PHQ Cards (set of 4)		1·50	3·50	☐	☐
	Set of 4 Gutter Pairs		2·00		☐	
	Set of 4 Traffic Light Gutter Pairs		3·00		☐	

Collectors Pack 1978

1978 (22 Nov.) *Comprises Nos.* 1050/7, 1059/74

	Collectors Pack	7·00		☐

555 Old English Sheepdog

556 Welsh Springer Spaniel

557 West Highland Terrier **558** Irish Setter

Dogs

1979 (7 Feb.) 'All-over' phosphor

1075	555	9p multicoloured	..	20	25	☐	☐
1076	556	10½p multicoloured	..	30	35	☐	☐
1077	557	11p multicoloured	..	35	40	☐	☐
1078	558	13p multicoloured	..	40	40	☐	☐
		Set of 4	.. .. ..	1·10	1·25	☐	☐
		First Day Cover	.. .. ..		1·40	☐	
		Presentation Pack	.. .. ..	1·50		☐	
		PHQ Cards (set of 4)	..	3·00	3·50	☐	☐
		Set of 4 Gutter Pairs	.. ..	2·25		☐	
		Set of 4 Traffic Light Gutter Pairs	.. .. ..	3·75		☐	

559 Primrose

561 Bluebell

560 Daffodil

562 Snowdrop

Spring Wild Flowers

1979 (21 Mar.) 'All-over' phosphor

1079	559	9p multicoloured	..	20	20	☐	☐
1080	560	10½p multicoloured	..	30	35	☐	☐
1081	561	11p multicoloured	..	35	40	☐	☐
1082	562	13p multicoloured	..	40	40	☐	☐
		Set of 4	.. .. ..	1·10	1·10	☐	☐
		First Day Cover	.. ..		1·25	☐	
		Presentation Pack	.. ..	1·50		☐	
		PHQ Cards (set of 4)	..	1·25	3·50	☐	☐
		Set of 4 Gutter Pairs	.. ..	2·25		☐	
		Set of 4 Traffic Light Gutter Pairs	.. .. ..	3·75		☐	

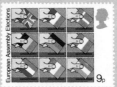

563

564

565

566

T **563/6** show hands placing the flags of the member nations into ballot boxes.

First Direct Elections to European Assembly

1979 (9 May) Phosphorised paper

1083	563	9p multicoloured	..	20	20	☐	☐
1084	564	10½p multicoloured	..	30	35	☐	☐
1085	565	11p multicoloured	..	35	40	☐	☐
1086	566	13p multicoloured	..	35	40	☐	☐
		Set of 4	.. .. ..	1·10	1·10	☐	☐
		First Day Cover	.. ..		1·25	☐	
		Presentation Pack	.. ..	1·50		☐	
		PHQ Cards (set of 4)	..	1·25	3·50	☐	☐
		Set of 4 Gutter Pairs	.. ..	2·25		☐	
		Set of 4 Traffic Light Gutter Pairs	.. ..	3·75		☐	

567 'Saddling "Mahmoud" for the Derby, 1936' (Sir Alfred Munnings)

568 'The Liverpool Great National Steeple Chase, 1839' (aquatint by F. C. Turner)

569 'The First Spring Meeting, Newmarket, 1793' (J. N. Sartorius)

570 'Racing at Dorsett Ferry, Windsor, 1684' (Francis Barlow)

INTRODUCING RUSHSTAMPS

FOR ALL YOUR G.B. REQUIREMENTS 1840 TO DATE (MINT, USED, FDC'S PRES. PACKS, BOOKLETS, ETC., ETC.). OUR "RUSH EXPRESS", 64 PAGE PRICE LIST COVERS JUST ABOUT EVERYTHING FOR THE BEGINNER AND THE MORE SERIOUS COLLECTOR. IT'S FREE ON REQUEST. OUR PRICES ARE VERY COMPETITIVE BACKED BY EXCELLENT STOCKS AND GOOD SERVICE! MAY WE SERVE YOU? WE SELL EVERY STAMP THAT IS LISTED IN THIS CATALOGUE. TELEPHONE & CREDIT CARD ORDERS WELCOMED.

TOP TWENTY OFFERS!

We guarantee delivery at these prices until the next edition of 'Collect British Stamps' is published in November 1991 or we will refund double the cost. (only 1 of each item can be ordered at these prices) Please order by Reference No.

ALL UNMOUNTED MINT UNLESS STATED OTHERWISE

Ref No.		Price
CBS01	1989 Greetings – complete set of 5 used	£1.20
CBS02	1988 Castles – £1, £1.50, £2 and £5 used	£1.99
CBS03	1939 G. VI 2/6 Brown and 10/- Blue, used	£5.50
CBS04	1840 1d Black – Spacefiller quality, used	£12.00
CBS05	1840 1d Black – Good used with 4 Margins	£44.00
CBS06	1840 2d Blue – Spacefiller, very high Catalogue Value, used	£17.00
CBS07	1960 Scotland 3d 2 Phosphor Bands, scarce stamps	£6.50
CBS08	1858 1d Red Plate No. Collection (Nos. 71 to 224, ex. 77) 150 stamps, all good/ fine used	£169.00
CBS09	1953 Coronation Set of 4, fine used	£3.75
CBS10	1963 I.O.M. 3d on Chalky Paper	£7.95
CBS11	1984 Frames ½p-17p Complete (34 values)	£15.00
CBS12	1971 Machin ½p Sideband, X842, fine used	£15.00
CBS13	1982 Postage Dues 1p to £5 (12 stamps) used	£1.95
CBS14	1988 Edward Lear S/sheet, fine used (scarce)	£5.00
CBS15	1983 Machin £1.30 on Official FDC	£4.50
CBS16	1983 Machin £1.30 Scarce Traffic Light Gutter Pair (normally £15.00)	£12.50
CBS17	1977/87 Machin £1 to £5 (8 values) Complete	£27.50
CBS18	do. as above Complete set sound used	£6.95
CBS19	1960 Phosphor ½d to 1/6 (17 values)	£3.50
CBS20	1847 Embossed 6d and 1/- values, used Spacefillers	£15.00

 RUSHSTAMPS (RETAIL) LTD, PO BOX 1, LYNDHURST, HANTS. SO43 7PP
(POSTAL ONLY) **TEL: (0703) 282044   FAX: (0703) 282981**

GB HIGH VALUES

SG	VALUE	UNMTD MINT	MTD MINT	FINE USED	SOUND USED
179	2/6	£160.00	£75.00	£16.00	£6.95
181	5/-	£360.00	£185.00	£24.00	£9.95
183	10/-	£540.00	£285.00	£95.00	£39.00
185	£1	POR	POR	£375.00	£220.00
186	£1	POR	POR	£580.00	£360.00
212	£1	POR	£795.00	£170.00	£110.00
316	2/6	£140.00	£60.00	£16.00	£8.95
263	5/-	£195.00	£80.00	£24.00	£9.95
265	10/-	£390.00	£180.00	£95.00	£46.00
320	£1	£690.00	£420.00	£160.00	£110.00
413a	2/6	£80.00	£32.00	£7.00	£1.95
416	5/-	£145.00	£75.00	£10.00	£2.95
417	10/-	£250.00	£140.00	£45.00	£18.00
403	£1	£1200.00	£740.00	£430.00	£250.00
438	£1	£550.00	£330.00	£325.00	£225.00
450	2/6	£58.00	£26.00	£2.95	£1.25
451	5/-	£120.00	£55.00	£12.50	£3.95
452	10/-	£250.00	£135.00	£19.50	£10.50
Set 3 Values		£420.00	£199.00	£30.00	£14.50
476	2/6	£22.50	£9.50	£3.50	£1.25
476a	2/6	£5.00	£2.50	£0.10	£0.10
477	5/-	£11.00	£5.00	£0.60	£0.30
478	10/-	£89.00	£52.00	£8.95	£4.50
478a	10/-	£22.00	£9.50	£1.25	£0.50
478b	£1	£10.50	£7.50	£8.50	£5.95
Set 6 Values		£149.00	£79.00	£25.00	£12.50
494	£1	£26.00	£22.00	£22.00	£14.00
509	2/6	£5.50	£2.00	£0.25	£0.10
510	5/-	£14.50	£6.00	£0.55	£0.20
511	10/-	£9.50	£6.90	£2.50	£0.95
512	£1	£16.00	£12.00	£8.50	£3.95
Set 4 Values		£44.00	£24.00	£11.50	£4.95
536	2/6	£5.75	£2.50	£0.50	£0.25
537	5/-	£24.00	£8.00	£1.50	£0.50
538	10/-	£48.00	£22.00	£6.50	£1.50
539	£1	£66.00	£30.00	£12.50	£4.95
Set 4 Values		£140.00	£58.00	£20.00	£7.00
595a	2/6	£0.12	£0.10	£0.10	£0.03
595k	2/6	£0.12	£0.10	£0.15	£0.10
596a	5/-	£0.45	£0.30	£0.20	£0.05
597a	10/-	£1.50	£0.95	£0.90	£0.60
598a	£1	£5.50	£4.50	£2.50	£1.20
Set 4 Values		£6.75	£5.00	£3.50	£1.50
759	2/6	£0.14	£0.10	£0.15	£0.05
760	5/-	£0.40	£0.25	£0.30	£0.12
761	10/-	£2.75	£2.20	£3.30	£1.00
762	£1	£1.90	£1.50	£2.00	£1.25
Set 4 Values		£4.75	£3.90	£3.95	£2.40
787	2/6	£0.25	£0.08	£0.10	£0.04
788	5/-	£1.20	£0.80	£0.25	£0.10
789	10/-	£3.50	£3.00	£3.50	£2.20
790	£1	£1.90	£1.40	£0.60	£0.30
Set 4 Values		£5.95	£4.50	£4.40	£2.60
829	10p	£0.55	£0.40	£0.30	£0.15
830	20p	£0.35	–	£0.08	£0.04
831	50p	£0.75	–	£0.15	£0.06
831a	£1	£1.75	–	£0.25	£0.10
Set 4 Values		£3.40	–	£0.75	£0.35

SG	VALUE	UNMTD MINT	GUTTER	T/L	FINE USED	SOUND USED
1026	£1	£1.50	£3.50	£4.00	£0.12	£0.05
1026b	£1.30	£4.95	£12.50	£15.00	£5.50	£2.50
1026c	£1.33	£4.50	£9.50	£14.50	£3.60	£1.50
1026d	£1.41	£4.20	£8.50	£10.50	£3.20	£1.50
1026e	£1.50	£2.90	£6.50	£8.00	£2.50	£0.85
1026f	£1.60	£2.90	£6.50	£8.00	£2.50	£0.95
1027	£2	£3.00	£6.50	£8.00	£0.25	£0.12
1028	£5	£7.50	£16.00	£20.00	£1.40	£0.75
Set 8 Values		£27.50	£68.00	£85.00	£17.95	£6.95
1410	£1.00	£1.40	–		£0.30	£0.10
1411	£1.50	£2.10	–		£0.50	£0.25
1412	£2.00	£2.75	–		£0.60	£0.30
1413	£5.00	£6.90	–		£2.50	£1.50
Set 4 Values		£13.00	–		£3.75	£1.99

ALL STAMPS SUPPLIED ARE OF THE FINEST QUALITY
FULL REFUND IF DISSATISFIED
ENQUIRIES INVITED FOR EARLIER VALUES AND VERY FINE USED

GB DEFINITIVE SETS

	No.	U/M	M/M	F/U	USED
1883 Lilac & Green ½d to 1/-..	(10v)	–	£675.00	–	£150.00
1887 Jubilee ½d to 1/-	(14v)	£310.00	£180.00	£70.00	£29.50
1902 Edward VII ½ to 1/-........	(15v)	£185.00	£95.00	£39.00	£18.95
1911 Edward VII 15–14...........	(5v)	£89.00	£45.00	£24.00	£12.00
1911/12 Downey Heads...........	(10v)	£69.00	£39.00	£28.00	£14.00
1912 GV Royal Cypher ½d to 1/-	(14v)	£85.00	£39.00	£21.00	£7.50
1912 6d perf 14.........................	(1v)	£65.00	£44.00	£48.00	£28.00
1912 9d Olive...........................	(1v)	£85.00	£40.00	£12.00	£5.50
1913 Mult. Cypher ½d & 1d ...	(2v)	£220.00	£120.00	£120.00	£89.00
1918 Bradbury 2/6, 5/-, 10/-......	(3v)	£425.00	£210.00	£68.00	£20.00
1924 GV Block Cypher ½d to 1/-	(12v)	£85.00	£39.00	£13.50	£6.95
1934 GV Photogravure ½d to 1/-	(11v)	£39.00	£18.95	£7.50	£2.95
1934 ReEngraved 2/6 to 10/-....	(3v)	£420.00	£199.00	£30.00	£14.50
1936 Edward VIII.....................	(4v)	£0.30	£0.20	£0.40	£0.18
1937 GVI Dark Colours...........	(15v)	£18.50	£8.95	£3.50	£1.50
1939 GVI 2/6 to £1	(6v)	£149.00	£75.00	£24.00	£12.00
1941 GVI Light ½d 3d............	(6v)	£1.30	£0.95	£0.80	£0.35
1950 GVI Colour Change	(6v)	£1.00	–	£0.95	£0.40
1951 Festivals 2/6 to £1...........	(4v)	£44.00	£24.00	£11.50	£4.95
1952 Tudor Watermark ½d to 1/6............	(17v)	£55.00	£19.50	£16.00	£7.50
1955 St. Edward Watermark ½d to 1/6............	(18v)	£75.00	£32.00	£12.50	£5.50
1955 Waterlow 2/6 to £1..........	(4v)	£140.00	£55.00	£20.00	£7.00
1957 Graphite (1st) ½d to 3d ..	(6v)	£5.95	£3.95	£3.95	£2.95
1958 Mult. Crowns ½d to 1/6 .	(17v)	£4.75	–	£1.75	£0.50
1958 2nd Graphite ½d to 4½d.	(8v)	£59.00	£42.00	£45.00	£32.00
1958 3d Graphite Error (592a) .	(1v)	£250.00	£150.00	£150.00	£95.00
1959 Phos. Graphite ½d to 4½d............	(8v)	£44.00	£32.00	£34.00	–
1959 2d Error (605a)	(1v)	£110.00	£85.00	£79.00	£59.00
1960 Mult. Crown Phos. ½d to 1/6............	(17v)	£3.95	–	£4.50	–
1960 Mult. Crown Phos. ½d to 1/6............	(24v)	£37.00	–	£29.50	–
1963 Bradbury 2/6 to £1..........	(4v)	£6.75	£5.00	£3.50	£1.80
1963 Chalky Paper 2/6............	(1v)	£0.12	–	£0.15	–
1967 Bradbury Unwatermarked 2/6 to £1.......	(4v)	£4.95	£3.90	£3.95	£2.40
1967 Machin ½d to 1/9...........	(16v)	£1.75	–	£1.50	£0.50
1967 Machin ½ to 1/9 All Types	(33v)	£5.95	–	–	–
1967 Machin 1d to 1/9 Gum Arabic............	(10v)	£1.75	–	–	–
1969 Machin 2/6 to £1	(4v)	£5.95	£4.50	£4.40	£2.60
1970/2 Machin 10p to £1.........	(4v)	£3.60	–	£0.75	£0.35
1972 Machin £1 Redrawn	(1v)	£1.75	–	–	–
1973 Machin 50p All Over Phos............	(1v)	£1.35	–	–	–
1977/87 High Values to £5 (incl. £1.30, £1.33, £1.41, £1.50, £1.60)............	(8v)	£28.50	–	–£17.95	£7.25
1984 Frames Complete ½p to 16p............	(32v)	£15.00	–	£17.50	–
1984 Frames 3½p, 12½p, 16p..	(3v)	£1.50	–	£1.95	–
1984 Frames 16½p and 17p.....	(2v)	£1.50	–	£1.95	–
1984 Frames 1st Class 'Unspecified' Value.............	(1v)	£7.50	–	£8.00	£6.00
1988 Castles to £5....................	(4v)	£13.00	–	£3.75	£1.99

Sideways and Inverted Watermarks available on request. Send for complete price list of sets and odd values.

RUSHSTAMPS (RETAIL) LTD, PO BOX 1, LYNDHURST, HANTS. SO43 7PP

(POSTAL ONLY) **TEL: (0703) 282044 FAX: (0703) 282981**

Horseracing Paintings and Bicentenary of The Derby (9p)

1979 (6 June) *'All-over' phosphor*

1087	**567**	9p multicoloured	..	25	25	☐	☐
1088	**568**	10½p multicoloured	..	30	30	☐	☐
1089	**569**	11p multicoloured	..	35	50	☐	☐
1090	**570**	13p multicoloured	..	40	55	☐	☐
	Set of 4	.. ..		1·10	1·40	☐	☐
	First Day Cover	.. ..			1·50		☐
	Presentation Pack	..		1·50		☐	
	PHQ Cards (set of 4)	..		1·25	3·00	☐	☐
	Set of 4 Gutter Pairs	..		2·25		☐	
	Set of 4 Traffic Light Gutter Pairs	..		3·75		☐	

571 *The Tale of Peter Rabbit* (Beatrix Potter)

572 *The Wind in the Willows* (Kenneth Grahame)

573 *Winnie-the-Pooh* (A. A. Milne)

574 *Alice's Adventures in Wonderland* (Lewis Carroll)

T **571/4** depict original illustrations from the four books.

International Year of the Child

1979 (11 July) *'All-over' phosphor*

1091	**571**	9p multicoloured	..	45	20	☐	☐
1092	**572**	10½p multicoloured	..	50	35	☐	☐
1093	**573**	11p multicoloured	..	55	40	☐	☐
1094	**574**	13p multicoloured	..	60	55	☐	☐
	Set of 4	.. ..		1·90	1·40	☐	☐
	First Day Cover	.. ..			1·40		☐
	Presentation Pack	..		2·25		☐	
	PHQ Cards (set of 4)	..		1·75	2·25	☐	☐
	Set of 4 Gutter Pairs	.. ..		4·00		☐	
	Set of 4 Traffic Light Gutter Pairs	.. ..		4·50		☐	

For full information on all future British issues, collectors should write to the British Post Office Philatelic Bureau, 20 Brandon Street, Edinburgh EH3 5TT

575 Sir Rowland Hill, 1795–1879

576 General Post, c. 1839

577 London Post, c. 1839

578 Uniform Postage, 1840

Death Centenary of Sir Rowland Hill (Postal Reformer)

1979 (22 Aug.–24 Oct.) *'All-over' phosphor*

1095	**575**	10p multicoloured	..	25	25	☐	☐
1096	**576**	11½p multicoloured	..	30	35	☐	☐
1097	**577**	13p multicoloured	..	35	40	☐	☐
1098	**578**	15p multicoloured	..	40	40	☐	☐
	Set of 4	.. ..		1·10	1·25	☐	☐
	First Day Cover	..			1·25		☐
	Presentation Pack	..		1·60		☐	
	PHQ Cards (set of 4)	..		1·25	2·25	☐	☐
	Set of 4 Gutter Pairs	..		2·40		☐	
	Set of 4 Traffic Light Gutter Pairs	.. .. ..		3·75		☐	
MS1099	89×121 mm. Nos. 1095/8			1·10	1·25	☐	☐
	First Day Cover (24 Oct.)	..			1·25		☐

No. **MS**1099 was sold at 59½p, the premium being used for the London 1980 Stamp Exhibition.

579 Policeman on the Beat

580 Policeman directing Traffic

55

13ᴾ

15ᴾ

581 Mounted Policewoman

582 River Patrol Boat

150th Anniversary of Metropolitan Police

1979 (26 Sᴇᴘᴛ.) *Phosphorised paper*

1100	**579**	10p multicoloured ..	25	25	☐	☐
1101	**580**	11½p multicoloured ..	30	35	☐	☐
1102	**581**	13p multicoloured ..	35	40	☐	☐
1103	**582**	15p multicoloured ..	40	40	☐	☐
	Set of 4		1·10	1·25	☐	☐
	First Day Cover			1·25		☐
	Presentation Pack		1·60		☐	
	PHQ Cards (set of 4)		1·25	2·25	☐	☐
	Set of 4 Gutter Pairs		2·40		☐	
	Set of 4 Traffic Light					
	Gutter Pairs		3·75		☐	

8ᴾ

10ᴾ

583 The Three Kings

584 Angel appearing to the Shepherds

11½ᴾ

13ᴾ

585 The Nativity

586 Mary and Joseph travelling to Bethlehem

15ᴾ

587 The Annunciation

Christmas

1979 (21 Nov.) *One centre phosphor band (8p) or phosphorised paper (others)*

1104	**583**	8p multicoloured ..	20	20	☐	☐
1105	**584**	10p multicoloured ..	25	25	☐	☐
1106	**585**	11½p multicoloured ..	30	35	☐	☐
1107	**586**	13p multicoloured ..	40	40	☐	☐
1108	**587**	15p multicoloured ..	40	45	☐	☐
	Set of 5		1·40	1·50	☐	☐
	First Day Cover			1·50		☐
	Presentation Pack		1·75		☐	
	PHQ Cards (set of 5)		1·25	2·25	☐	☐
	Set of 5 Gutter Pairs		3·00		☐	
	Set of 5 Traffic Light					
	Gutter Pairs		3·75		☐	

Collectors Pack 1979

1979 (21 Nov.) *Comprises Nos.* 1075/98, 1100/8

Collectors Pack	9·00		☐

588 Kingfisher

589 Dipper

590 Moorhen

591 Yellow Wagtails

Centenary of Wild Bird Protection Act

1980 (16 Jᴀɴ.) *Phosphorised paper*

1109	**588**	10p multicoloured ..	25	25	☐	☐
1110	**589**	11½p multicoloured ..	30	35	☐	☐
1111	**590**	13p multicoloured ..	40	45	☐	☐
1112	**591**	15p multicoloured ..	45	50	☐	☐
	Set of 4		1·25	1·40	☐	☐
	First Day Cover			1·40		☐
	Presentation Pack		1·75		☐	
	PHQ Cards (set of 4)		1·25	2·25	☐	☐
	Set of 4 Gutter Pairs		2·50		☐	

592 *Rocket* approaching Moorish Arch, Liverpool

593 First and Second Class Carriages passing through Olive Mount Cutting

594 Third Class Carriage and Cattle Truck crossing Chat Moss

595 Horsebox and Carriage Truck near Bridgewater Canal

596 Goods Truck and Mail-coach at Manchester

T **592/6** were printed together, *se-tenant* in horizontal strips of 5 throughout the sheet.

150th Anniversary of Liverpool and Manchester Railway

1980 (12 MAR.) *Phosphorised paper*

1113	**592**	12p multicoloured	25	25	☐	☐
		a. Strip of 5.				
		Nos. 1113/17	1·50	1·60	☐	☐
1114	**593**	12p multicoloured	25	25	☐	☐
1115	**594**	12p multicoloured	25	25	☐	☐
1116	**595**	12p multicoloured	25	25	☐	☐
1117	**596**	12p multicoloured	25	25	☐	☐
		Set of 5	1·50	1·10	☐	☐
		First Day Cover		1·60		☐
		Presentation Pack	2·00		☐	
		PHQ Cards (set of 5)	1·25	3·00	☐	☐
		Gutter strip of 10	3·25		☐	

597 Montage of London Buildings

"London 1980" International Stamp Exhibition

1980 (9 APR–7 MAY) *Phosphorised paper. Perf* $14\frac{1}{2} \times 14$

1118	**597**	50p agate			1·50	1·50	☐	☐
		First Day Cover				1·50		☐
		Presentation Pack			1·75		☐	
		PHQ Card			50	1·50	☐	☐
		Gutter Pair			3·00		☐	
MS1119	90 × 123 mm. No. 1118				1·50	1·50	☐	☐
		First Day Cover (7 May)				1·50		☐

No. **MS**1119 was sold at 75p, the premium being used for the exhibition.

598 Buckingham Palace

599 The Albert Memorial

600 Royal Opera House

601 Hampton Court

17½p Kensington Palace **602** Kensington Palace

607 Queen Elizabeth the Queen Mother

London Landmarks

1980 (7 MAY) *Phosphorised paper*

1120	**598**	10½p multicoloured	25	25	☐	☐
1121	**599**	12p multicoloured	30	30	☐	☐
1122	**600**	13½p multicoloured	35	35	☐	☐
1123	**601**	15p multicoloured	40	45	☐	☐
1124	**602**	17½p multicoloured	50	55	☐	☐
		Set of 5	1·60	1·75	☐	☐
		First Day Cover		1·75		☐
		Presentation Pack	2·10		☐	
		PHQ Cards (set of 5)	1·25	2·50	☐	☐
		Set of 5 Gutter Pairs	3·50		☐	

80th Birthday of Queen Elizabeth the Queen Mother

1980 (4 AUG.) *Phosphorised paper*

1129	**607**	12p multicoloured	50	50	☐	☐
		First Day Cover		60		☐
		PHQ Card	50	90	☐	☐
		Gutter Pair	1·00		☐	

603 Charlotte Bronte (*Jane Eyre*)

604 George Eliot (*The Mill on the Floss*)

608 Sir Henry Wood

609 Sir Thomas Beecham

605 Emily Bronte (*Wuthering Heights*)

606 Mrs Gaskell (*North and South*)

T **603/6** show authoresses and scenes from their novels. T **603/4** also include the "Europa" C.E.P.T. emblem.

610 Sir Malcolm Sargent

611 Sir John Barbirolli

Famous Authoresses

1980 (9 JULY) *Phosphorised paper*

1125	**603**	12p multicoloured	30	30	☐	☐
1126	**604**	13½p multicoloured	35	35	☐	☐
1127	**605**	15p multicoloured	40	45	☐	☐
1128	**606**	17½p multicoloured	60	60	☐	☐
		Set of 4	1·50	1·50	☐	☐
		First Day Cover		1·50		☐
		Presentation Pack	1·90		☐	
		PHQ Cards (set of 4)	1·25	2·00	☐	☐
		Set of 4 Gutter Pairs	3·25		☐	

British Conductors

1980 (10 SEPT.) *Phosphorised paper*

1130	**608**	12p multicoloured	30	30	☐	☐
1131	**609**	13½p multicoloured	35	40	☐	☐
1132	**610**	15p multicoloured	45	45	☐	☐
1133	**611**	17½p multicoloured	55	50	☐	☐
		Set of 4	1·50	1·50	☐	☐
		First Day Cover		1·50		☐
		Presentation Pack	1·90		☐	
		PHQ Cards (set of 4)	1·50	2·00	☐	☐
		Set of 4 Gutter Pairs	3·25		☐	

612 Running

613 Rugby

614 Boxing

615 Cricket

Sports Centenaries

1980 (10 Oct.) *Phosphorised paper. Perf* 14 × 14½

1134	**612**	12p multicoloured ..	30	30	□	□
1135	**613**	13½p multicoloured ..	35	40	□	□
1136	**614**	15p multicoloured ..	40	40	□	□
1137	**615**	17½p multicoloured ..	60	55	□	□
		Set of 4	1·50	1·50	□	□
		First Day Cover		1·50		□
		Presentation Pack	1·90		□	
		PHQ Cards (set of 4)	1·25	2·00	□	□
		Set of 4 Gutter Pairs ..	3·25		□	

Centenaries:— 12p Amateur Athletics Association; 13½p Welsh Rugby Union; 15p Amateur Boxing Association; 17½p First England v Australia Test Match.

616 Christmas Tree

617 Candles

618 Apples and Mistletoe

619 Crown, Chains and Bell

620 Holly

Christmas

1980 (19 Nov.) *One centre phosphor band (10p) or phosphorised paper (others)*

1138	**616**	10p multicoloured ..	25	25	□	□
1139	**617**	12p multicoloured ..	30	35	□	□
1140	**618**	13½p multicoloured ..	35	40	□	□
1141	**619**	15p multicoloured ..	40	45	□	□
1142	**620**	17½p multicoloured ..	45	50	□	□
		Set of 5	1·60	1·75	□	□
		First Day Cover		1·75		□
		Presentation Pack	2·10		□	
		PHQ Cards (set of 5)	1·25	2·00	□	□
		Set of 5 Gutter Pairs ..	3·50		□	

Collectors Pack 1980

1980 (19 Nov.) *Comprises Nos.* 1109/18, 1120/42

	Collectors Pack	13·00	□

621 St. Valentine's Day

622 Morris Dancers

623 Lammastide

624 Medieval Mummers

T **621/22** also include the "Europa" C.E.P.T. emblem.

Folklore

1981 (6 FEB.) *Phosphorised paper*

1143	**621**	14p multicoloured ..	35	35	☐	☐
1144	**622**	18p multicoloured ..	45	50	☐	☐
1145	**623**	22p multicoloured ..	60	60	☐	☐
1146	**624**	25p multicoloured ..	75	70	☐	☐
		Set of 4	2·00	2·00	☐	☐
		First Day Cover ..		2·00		☐
		Presentation Pack	2·40		☐	
		PHQ Cards (set of 4) ..	1·50	2·00	☐	☐
		Set of 4 Gutter Pairs	4·00		☐	

625 Blind Man with Guide Dog

626 Hands spelling "Deaf" in Sign Language

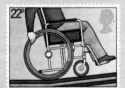

627 Disabled Man in Wheelchair

628 Disabled Artist painting with Foot

International Year of the Disabled

1981 (25 MAR.) *Phosphorised paper*

1147	**625**	14p multicoloured ..	35	35	☐	☐
1148	**626**	18p multicoloured ..	45	50	☐	☐
1149	**627**	22p multicoloured ..	60	60	☐	☐
1150	**628**	25p multicoloured ..	75	70	☐	☐
		Set of 4	2·00	2·00	☐	☐
		First Day Cover		2·00		☐
		Presentation Pack	2·40		☐	
		PHQ Cards (set of 4) ..	1·50	2·25	☐	☐
		Set of 4 Gutter Pairs	4·00		☐	

629 Small Tortoiseshell

630 Large Blue

631 Peacock

632 Chequered Skipper

Butterflies

1981 (13 MAY) *Phosphorised paper*

1151	**629**	14p multicoloured ..	35	35	☐	☐
1152	**630**	18p multicoloured ..	50	50	☐	☐
1153	**631**	22p multicoloured ..	60	65	☐	☐
1154	**632**	25p multicoloured ..	70	75	☐	☐
		Set of 4	2·00	2·00	☐	☐
		First Day Cover		2·00		☐
		Presentation Pack	2·50		☐	
		PHQ Cards (set of 4) ..	1·60	2·25	☐	☐
		Set of 4 Gutter Pairs ..	4·00		☐	

633 Glenfinnan, Scotland

634 Derwentwater, England

635 Stackpole Head, Wales

636 Giant's Causeway, N. Ireland

637 St Kilda, Scotland

50th Anniversary of National Trust for Scotland

1981 (24 JUNE) *Phosphorised paper*

1155	**633**	14p multicoloured ..	40	40	□	□
1156	**634**	18p multicoloured ..	50	55	□	☑
1157	**635**	20p multicoloured ..	55	60	□	□
1158	**636**	22p multicoloured ..	60	60	□	□
1159	**637**	25p multicoloured ..	75	70	□	□
		Set of 5	2·50	2·50	□	□
		First Day Cover..		2·50		□
		Presentation Pack	2·90		□	
		PHQ Cards (set of 5) ..	2·00	2·75	□	□
		Set of 5 Gutter Pairs	5·00		□	

638 Prince Charles and Lady Diana Spencer

Royal Wedding

1981 (22 JULY) *Phosphorised paper*

1160	**638**	14p multicoloured ..	35	35	□	□
1161		25p multicoloured ..	90	90	□	□
		Set of 2	1·25	1·25	□	□
		First Day Cover		2·00		□
		Presentation Pack ..	1·75		□	
		Souvenir Book	4·50		□	
		PHQ Cards (set of 2) ..	1·00	2·00	□	□
		Set of 2 Gutter Pairs ..	2·50		□	

639 "Expeditions"

640 "Skills"

641 "Service"

642 "Recreation"

25th Anniversary of Duke of Edinburgh Award Scheme

1981 (12 AUG.) *Phosphorised paper. Perf 14*

1162	**639**	14p multicoloured ..	35	35	□	□
1163	**640**	18p multicoloured ..	50	50	□	□
1164	**641**	22p multicoloured ..	60	60	□	□
1165	**642**	25p multicoloured ..	70	70	□	□
		Set of 4	2·00	2·00	□	□
		First Day Cover.. ..		2·00		□
		Presentation Pack ..	2·50		□	
		PHQ Cards (set of 4)	1·60	2·25	□	□
		Set of 4 Gutter Pairs	4·00		□	

643 Cockle-Dredging

644 Hauling Trawl Net

645 Lobster Potting

646 Hoisting Seine Net

Fishing Industry

1981 (23 SEPT.) *Phosphorised paper*

1166	**643**	14p multicoloured ..	35	35	□	□
1167	**644**	18p multicoloured ..	50	50	□	□
1168	**645**	22p multicoloured ..	60	60	□	□
1169	**646**	25p multicoloured ..	70	65	□	□
		Set of 4	2·00	2·00	□	□
		First Day Cover..		2·00		□
		Presentation Pack	2·50		□	
		PHQ Cards (set of 4) ..	1·75	2·25	□	□
		Set of 4 Gutter Pairs	4·00		□	

Nos. 1166/9 were issued on the occasion of the centenary of Royal National Mission to Deep Sea Fishermen.

647 Father Christmas

648 Jesus Christ

649 Flying Angel

650 Joseph and Mary arriving at Bethlehem

651 Three Kings approaching Bethlehem

652 Charles Darwin and Giant Tortoises

653 Darwin and Marine Iguanas

654 Darwin, Cactus Ground Finch and Large Ground Finch

655 Darwin and Prehistoric Skulls

Death Centenary of Charles Darwin

1982 (10 Feb.) *Phosphorised paper*

1175	**652**	15½p multicoloured	..	35	35	☐	☐
1176	**653**	19½p multicoloured	..	60	60	☐	☐
1177	**654**	26p multicoloured	..	70	70	☐	☐
1178	**655**	29p multicoloured	..	75	75	☐	☐
		Set of 4		2·25	2·25	☐	☐
		First Day Cover			2·25		☐
		Presentation Pack		2·60		☐	
		PHQ Cards (set of 4) ..		2·25	4·50	☐	☐
		Set of 4 Gutter Pairs		4·75		☐	

656 Boys' Brigade

657 Girls' Brigade

658 Boy Scout Movement

659 Girl Guide Movement

Christmas. Children's Pictures

1981 (18 Nov.) *One phosphor band (11½p) or phosphorised paper (others)*

1170	**647**	11½p multicoloured	..	30	30	☐	☐
1171	**648**	14p multicoloured	..	40	40	☐	☐
1172	**649**	18p multicoloured	..	50	50	☐	☐
1173	**650**	22p multicoloured	..	60	60	☐	☐
1174	**651**	25p multicoloured	..	70	70	☐	☐
		Set of 5		2·25	2·25	☐	☐
		First Day Cover			2·25		☐
		Presentation Pack		2·60		☐	
		PHQ Cards (set of 5) ..		2·00	2·50	☐	☐
		Set of 5 Gutter Pairs ..		4·50		☐	

Collectors Pack 1981

1981 (18 Nov.) *Comprises Nos.* 1143/74

	Collectors Pack	20·00	☐	

For full information on all future British issues, collectors should write to the British Post Office Philatelic Bureau, 20 Brandon Street, Edinburgh EH3 5TT.

Youth Organizations

1982 (24 MAR.) *Phosphorised paper*

1179	**656**	15½p multicoloured	..	35	35	☐ ☐
1180	**657**	19½p multicoloured	..	70	70	☐ ☐
1181	**658**	26p multicoloured	..	90	90	☐ ☐
1182	**659**	29p multicoloured	..	1·00	1·00	☐ ☐
		Set of 4	.. .. ..	2·75	2·75	☐ ☐
		First Day Cover	.. .. ..		2·75	☐
		Presentation Pack	.. ..	3·25		☐
		PHQ Cards (set of 4)	.. ..	2·50	3·00	☐ ☐
		Set of 4 Gutter Pairs	.. ..	5·50		☐

Nos. 1179/82 were issued on the occasion of the 75th anniversary of the Boy Scout Movement, the 125th birth anniversary of Lord Baden-Powell and the centenary of the Boys' Brigade (1983).

660 Ballerina

661 'Harlequin'

662 'Hamlet'

663 Opera Singer

Europa. British Theatre

1982 (28 APR.) *Phosphorised paper*

1183	**660**	15½p multicoloured	..	35	35	☐ ☐
1184	**661**	19½p multicoloured	..	70	70	☐ ☐
1185	**662**	26p multicoloured	..	90	90	☐ ☐
1186	**663**	29p multicoloured	..	1·00	1·00	☐ ☐
		Set of 4	.. .. ..	2·75	2·75	☐ ☐
		First Day Cover	.. .. ..		2·75	☐
		Presentation Pack	.. ..	3·00		☐
		PHQ Cards (set of 4)	.. ..	2·50	3·00	☐ ☐
		Set of 4 Gutter Pairs	.. ..	5·50		☐

664 Henry VIII and *Mary Rose*

665 Admiral Blake and *Triumph*

666 Lord Nelson and HMS *Victory*

667 Lord Fisher and HMS *Dreadnought*

668 Viscount Cunningham and HMS *Warspite*

Maritime Heritage

1982 (16 JUNE) *Phosphorised paper*

1187	**664**	15½p multicoloured	..	35	35	☐ ☐
1188	**665**	19½p multicoloured	..	60	60	☐ ☐
1189	**666**	24p multicoloured	..	70	70	☐ ☐
1190	**667**	26p multicoloured	..	80	80	☐ ☐
1191	**668**	29p multicoloured	..	90	90	☐ ☐
		Set of 5	.. .. ..	3·00	3·00	☐ ☐
		First Day Cover	.. .. ..		3·00	☐
		Presentation Pack	.. ..	3·25		☐
		PHQ Cards (set of 5)	.. ..	3·00	3·50	☐ ☐
		Set of 5 Gutter Pairs	.. ..	6·00		☐

669 "Strawberry Thief" (William Morris)

670 Untitled (Steiner and Co)

671 "Cherry Orchard"
(Paul Nash)

672 "Chevron" (Andrew
Foster)

British Textiles

1982 (23 July) *Phosphorised paper*

1192	**669**	15½p multicoloured ..	35	35	☐	☐
1193	**670**	19½p multicoloured ..	70	70	☐	☐
1194	**671**	26p multicoloured ..	70	70	☐	☐
1195	**672**	29p multicoloured ..	1·00	1·00	☐	☐
		Set of 4	2·50	2·50	☐	☐
		First Day Cover		2·50		☐
		Presentation Pack	2·90		☐	
		PHQ Cards (set of 4)	2·50	3·50	☐	☐
		Set of 4 Gutter Pairs	5·00		☐	

   Nos 1192/5 were issued on the occasion of the 250th birth anniversary of Sir Richard Arkwright (inventor of spinning machine).

673 Development of Communications

674 Modern Technological Aids

Information Technology

1982 (8 Sept.) *Phosphorised paper. Perf* 14×15

1196	**673**	15½p multicoloured ..	45	50	☐	☐
1197	**674**	26p multicoloured ..	80	85	☐	☐
		Set of 2	1·25	1·25	☐	☐
		First Day Cover		1·50		☐
		Presentation Pack	1·75		☐	
		PHQ Cards (set of 2)	1·50	3·50	☐	☐
		Set of 2 Gutter Pairs	2·50		☐	

675 Austin "Seven" and "Metro"   **676** Ford "Model T" and "Escort"

677 Jaguar "SS1" and "XJ6"   **678** Rolls-Royce "Silver Ghost" and "Silver Spirit"

British Motor Industry

1982 (13 Oct.) *Phosphorised paper. Perf* 14½×14

1198	**675**	15½p multicoloured ..	50	50	☐	☐
1199	**676**	19½p multicoloured ..	1·00	1·10	☐	☐
1200	**677**	26p multicoloured ..	1·10	1·25	☐	☐
1201	**678**	29p multicoloured ..	1·25	1·40	☐	☐
		Set of 4	3·50	3·75	☐	☐
		First Day Cover		3·75		☐
		Presentation Pack	4·00		☐	
		PHQ Cards (set of 4)	2·60	4·50	☐	☐
		Set of 4 Gutter Pairs	7·00		☐	

679 "While Shepherds Watched"

680 "The Holly and the Ivy"

681 "I Saw Three Ships"

682 "We Three Kings"

683 "Good King Wenceslas"

Christmas. Carols

1982 (17 Nov.) *One phosphor band (12½p) or phosphorised paper (others)*

1202	**679**	12½p multicoloured	..	30	30	☐ ☐
1203	**680**	15½p multicoloured		55	55	☐ ☐
1204	**681**	19½p multicoloured		80	80	☐ ☐
1205	**682**	26p multicoloured		80	80	☐ ☐
1206	**683**	29p multicoloured		90	90	☐ ☐
		Set of 5	.. ..	3·00	3·00	☐
		First Day Cover	.. ..		3·00	☐
		Presentation Pack	..	3·50		☐
		PHQ Cards (set of 5)	..	2·75	4·50	☐ ☐
		Set of 5 Gutter Pairs	.. ..	6·00		☐

Collectors Pack 1982

1982 (17 Nov.) *Comprises Nos.* 1175/1206

	Collectors Pack	.. .. ..	27·00	☐

684 Salmon

685 Pike

686 Trout

687 Perch

British River Fishes

1983 (26 Jan.) *Phosphorised paper*

1207	**684**	15½p multicoloured	..	35	35	☐ ☐
1208	**685**	19½p multicoloured	..	70	70	☐ ☐
1209	**686**	26p multicoloured		80	80	☐ ☐
1210	**687**	29p multicoloured		90	90	☐ ☐
		Set of 4	.. .. ..	2·50	2·50	☐ ☐
		First Day Cover	.. ..		2·75	☐
		Presentation Pack	..	3·00		☐
		PHQ Cards (set of 4)	..	2·50	4·50	☐
		Set of 4 Gutter Pairs	.. ..	5·25		☐

688 Tropical Island

689 Desert

690 Temperate Farmland

691 Mountain Range

Commonwealth Day. Geographical Regions

1983 (9 Mar.) *Phosphorised paper*

1211	**688**	15½p multicoloured	..	35	35	☐ ☐
1212	**689**	19½p multicoloured	..	70	70	☐ ☐
1213	**690**	26p multicoloured	..	80	80	☐ ☐
1214	**691**	29p multicoloured	..	90	90	☐ ☐
		Set of 4	.. ..	2·50	2·50	☐ ☐
		First Day Cover	.. ..		2·75	☐
		Presentation Pack	..	3·00		☐
		PHQ Cards (set of 4)	..	2·50	4·50	☐ ☐
		Set of 4 Gutter Pairs	.. ..	5·25		☐

692 Humber Bridge

693 Thames Flood Barrier

694 *Iolair* (oilfield emergency support vessel)

Europa. Engineering Achievements

1983 (25 MAY) *Phosphorised paper.*

1215	**692**	16p multicoloured ..	55	55	☐	☐
1216	**693**	20½p multicoloured	1·25	1·25	☐	☐
1217	**694**	28p multicoloured	1·25	1·25	☐	☐
	Set of 3	2·75	2·75	☐	☐
	First Day Cover		2·75		☐
	Presentation Pack	3·50		☐	
	PHQ Cards (*set of 3*)	2·50	3·75	☐	☐
	Set of 3 Gutter Pairs	5·50		☐	

British Army Uniforms

1983 (6 JULY) *Phosphorised paper.*

1218	**695**	16p multicoloured ..	40	40	☐	☐
1219	**696**	20½p multicoloured ..	70	70	☐	☐
1220	**697**	26p multicoloured ..	80	80	☐	☐
1221	**698**	28p multicoloured ..	80	80	☐	☐
1222	**699**	31p multicoloured ..	90	90	☐	☐
	Set of 5	3·25	3·25	☐	☐
	First Day Cover		3·25		☐
	Presentation Pack	4·00		☐	
	PHQ Cards (*set of 5*)	4·00	5·00	☐	☐
	Set of 5 Gutter Pairs	6·50		☐	

Nos. 1218/22 were issued on the occasion of the 350th anniversary of The Royal Scots, the senior line regiment of the British Army.

695 Musketeer and Pikeman. The Royal Scots (1633)

696 Fusilier and Ensign. The Royal Welch Fusiliers (mid-18th century)

20TH CENTURY GARDEN SISSINGHURST

700 20th-Century Garden, Sissinghurst

19TH CENTURY GARDEN BIDDULPH GRANGE

701 19th-Century Garden, Biddulph Grange

697 Riflemen. 96th Rifles (The Royal Green Jackets) (1805)

698 Sergeant (khaki service uniform) and Guardsman (full dress). The Irish Guards (1900)

18TH CENTURY GARDEN BLENHEIM

702 18th-Century Garden, Blenheim

17TH CENTURY GARDEN PITMEDDEN

703 17th-Century Garden, Pitmedden

British Gardens

1983 (24 AUG.) *Phosphorised paper. Perf* 14

1223	**700**	16p multicoloured ..	40	40	☐	☐
1224	**701**	20½p multicoloured ..	50	55	☐	☐
1225	**702**	28p multicoloured ..	85	90	☐	☐
1226	**703**	31p multicoloured ..	90	90	☐	☐
	Set of 4	2·50	2·50	☐	☐
	First Day Cover		2·75		☐
	Presentation Pack	3·25		☐	
	PHQ Cards (*set of 4*)	2·50	4·50	☐	☐
	Set of 4 Gutter Pairs	5·00		☐	

699 Paratroopers. The Parachute Regiment (1983)

704 Merry-go-round

705 Big Wheel, Helter-skelter and Performing Animals

712 "Christmas Dove" (hedge sculpture)

706 Side-shows

707 Early Produce Fair

British Fairs

1983 (5 Oct.) *Phosphorised paper.*

1227	**704**	16p multicoloured	..	40	40	☐ ☐
1228	**705**	20½p multicoloured	..	50	55	☐ ☐
1229	**706**	28p multicoloured	..	85	90	☐ ☐
1230	**707**	31p multicoloured	..	90	90	☐ ☐
	Set of 4	.. .. ..	..	2·50	2·50	☐ ☐
	First Day Cover	.. ..			2·75	☐
	Presentation Pack	..		3·25		☐
	PHQ Cards (set of 4)	.. ..		2·50	4·50	☐ ☐
	Set of 4 Gutter Pairs	.. ..		5·00		☐

Nos. 1227/30 were issued to mark the 850th Anniversary of St. Bartholomew's Fair, Smithfield, London.

Christmas

1983 (16 Nov.) *One phosphor band (12½p) or phosphorised paper (others)*

1231	**708**	12½p multicoloured	..	30	30	☐ ☐
1232	**709**	16p multicoloured	..	45	45	☐ ☐
1233	**710**	20½p multicoloured	..	70	70	☐ ☐
1234	**711**	28p multicoloured	..	90	90	☐ ☐
1235	**712**	31p multicoloured	..	1·00	1·00	☐ ☐
	Set of 5	.. .. ..		3·00	3·00	☐ ☐
	First Day Cover	.. ..			3·00	☐
	Presentation Pack	..		3·50		☐
	PHQ Cards (set of 5)	.. ..		3·00	4·50	☐ ☐
	Set of 5 Gutter Pairs	.. ..		6·00		☐

Collectors Pack 1983

1983 (16 Nov.) *Comprises Nos.* 1207/35

	Collectors Pack	.. ..	45·00	☐

708 "Christmas Post" (pillar-box)

709 "The Three Kings" (chimney-pots)

713 Arms of the College of Arms

714 Arms of King Richard III (founder)

710 "World at Peace" (Dove and Blackbird)

711 "Light of Christmas" (street lamp)

715 Arms of the Earl Marshal of England

716 Arms of the City of London

500th Anniversary of College of Arms

1984 (17 Jan) *Phosphorised paper. Perf 14½*

1236	**713**	16p multicoloured ..	40	40	☐	☐
1237	**714**	20½p multicoloured ..	70	70	☐	☐
1238	**715**	28p multicoloured ..	95	95	☐	☐
1239	**716**	31p multicoloured ..	1·00	1·00	☐	☐
		Set of 4	2·75	2·75	☐	☐
		First Day Cover		3·00		☐
		Presentation Pack	3·25		☐	
		PHQ Cards (set of 4)	2·50	5·00	☐	☐
		Set of 4 Gutter Pairs	5·75		☐	

717 Highland Cow

718 Chillingham Wild Bull

719 Hereford Bull

720 Welsh Black Bull

721 Irish Moiled Cow

British Cattle

1984 (6 Mar.) *Phosphorised paper.*

1240	**717**	16p multicoloured ..	40	40	☐	☐
1241	**718**	20½p multicoloured ..	65	65	☐	☐
1242	**719**	26p multicoloured ..	70	70	☐	☐
1243	**720**	28p multicoloured ..	85	85	☐	☐
1244	**721**	31p multicoloured ..	1·00	1·00	☐	☐
		Set of 5	3·25	3·25	☐	☐
		First Day Cover		3·50		☐
		Presentation Pack	4·00		☐	
		PHQ Cards (set of 5)	3·00	5·00	☐	☐
		Set of 5 Gutter Pairs	6·50		☐	

Nos. 1240/4 marked the centenary of the Highland Cattle Society and the bicentenary of the Royal Highland and Agricultural Society of Scotland.

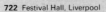

722 Festival Hall, Liverpool

723 Milburngate Shopping Centre, Durham

724 Bush House, Bristol

725 Commercial Street Housing Scheme, Perth

Urban Renewal

1984 (10 Apr.) *Phosphorised paper.*

1245	**722**	16p multicoloured ..	40	40	☐	☐
1246	**723**	20½p multicoloured ..	70	70	☐	☐
1247	**724**	28p multicoloured ..	95	95	☐	☐
1248	**725**	31p multicoloured ..	1·00	1·00	☐	☐
		Set of 4	2·75	2·75	☐	☐
		First Day Cover		3·00		☐
		Presentation Pack	3·25		☐	
		PHQ Cards (set of 4)	2·50	5·00	☐	☐
		Set of 4 Gutter Pairs	5·50		☐	

Nos. 1245/8 mark the opening of the International Gardens Festival, Liverpool, and the 150th anniversaries of the Royal Institute of British Architects and the Chartered Institute of Building.

726 C.E.P.T. 25th Anniversary Logo

727 Abduction of Europa

Nos. 1249/50 and 1251/2 were each printed together, *se-tenant*, in horizontal pairs throughout the sheets.

Europa. 25th Anniversary of C.E.P.T. and 2nd European Parliamentary Elections

1984 (15 May) *Phosphorised paper.*

1249	726	16p	greenish slate, dp blue and gold ..	40	60	☐	☐
		a.	*Horiz pair. Nos. 1249/50*	1·25	1·25	☐	☐
1250	727	16p	greenish slate, dp bl, blk and gold ..	40	60	☐	☐
1251	726	20½p	Venetian red, deep magenta and gold ..	70	90	☐	☐
		a.	*Horizontal pair. Nos. 1251/2*	1·75	1·75	☐	☐
1252	727	20½p	Venetian red, deep magenta, black and gold ..	70	90	☐	☐
			Set of 4 ..	2·75	2·75	☐	☐
			First Day Cover ..		3·00		☐
			Presentation Pack ..	3·25		☐	
			PHQ Cards (set of 4) ..	2·50	5·00	☐	☐
			Set of 4 Gutter Pairs ..	5·50		☐	

728 Lancaster House

London Economic Summit Conference

1984 (5 June) *Phosphorised paper.*

1253	728	31p	multicoloured ..	1·25	1·25	☐	☐
			First Day Cover ..		2·00		☐
			PHQ Card ..	50	1·60	☐	☐
			Gutter Pair ..	2·50			☐

729 View of Earth from "Apollo 11"

730 Navigational Chart of English Channel

731 Greenwich Observatory

732 Sir George Airey's Transit Telescope

Centenary of Greenwich Meridian

1984 (26 June) *Phosphorised paper. Perf 14 × 14½*

1254	729	16p	multicoloured ..	40	40	☐	☐
1255	730	20½p	multicoloured ..	60	60	☐	☐
1256	731	28p	multicoloured ..	95	95	☐	☐
1257	732	31p	multicoloured ..	1·10	1·10	☐	☐
			Set of 4 ..	2·75	2·75	☐	☐
			First Day Cover ..		2·75		☐
			Presentation Pack ..	3·25		☐	
			PHQ Cards (set of 4) ..	2·50	5·50	☐	☐
			Set of 4 Gutter Pairs ..	5·50		☐	

733 Bath Mail Coach, 1784

734 Attack on Exeter Mail, 1816

735 Norwich Mail in Thunderstorm, 1827

736 Holyhead and Liverpool Mails leaving London, 1828

737 Edinburgh Mail Snowbound, 1831

T **733/7** were printed together, *se-tenant* in horizontal strips of 5 throughout the sheet.

Bicentenary of First Mail Coach Run, Bath and Bristol to London

1984 (31 JULY) *Phosphorised paper*

1258	**733**	16p multicoloured	..	60	60	☐	☐
		a. *Horiz strip of 5.*					
		Nos. 1258/62	..	2·75	2·75	☐	☐
1259	**734**	16p multicoloured		60	60	☐	☐
1260	**735**	16p multicoloured		60	60	☐	☐
1261	**736**	16p multicoloured		60	60	☐	☐
1262	**737**	16p multicoloured		60	60	☐	☐
		Set of 5	..		2·75	2·75	☐	☐
		First Day Cover	.. ..		2·75		☐
		Presentation Pack ..		3·25		☐	
		Souvenir Book	.. ..	6·00		☐	
		PHQ Cards (set of 5)	..	3·00	5·00	☐	☐
		Gutter Strip of 10 ..	..	5·50		☐	

738 Nigerian Clinic

739 Violinist and Acropolis, Athens

740 Building Project, Sri Lanka

741 British Council Library

50th Anniversary of The British Council

1984 (25 SEPT.) *Phosphorised paper*

1263	**738**	17p multicoloured	..	50	50	☐	☐
1264	**739**	22p multicoloured		75	75	☐	☐
1265	**740**	31p multicoloured		1·10	1·10	☐	☐
1266	**741**	34p multicoloured		1·25	1·25	☐	☐
		Set of 4	.. ..	3·25	3·25	☐	☐
		First Day Cover			3·50		☐
		Presentation Pack	.. ..	3·50		☐	
		PHQ Cards (set of 4)		2·50	4·50	☐	☐
		Set of 4 Gutter Pairs		6·50		☐	

For full information on all future British issues, collectors should write to the British Post Office Philatelic Bureau, 20 Brandon Street, Edinburgh EH3 5TT.

742 The Holy Family

743 Arrival in Bethlehem

744 Shepherd and Lamb

745 Virgin and Child

746 Offering of Frankincense

Christmas

1984 (20 Nov.) *One phosphor band (13p) or phosphorised paper (others)*

1267	**742**	13p multicoloured	..	30	30	☐	☐
1268	**743**	17p multicoloured	..	40	45	☐	☐
1269	**744**	22p multicoloured	..	55	60	☐	☐
1270	**745**	31p multicoloured	..	1·00	1·10	☐	☐
1271	**746**	34p multicoloured	..	1·00	1·10	☐	☐
		Set of 5	.. ..	3·00	3·25	☐	☐
		First Day Cover	.. ..		3·25		☐
		Presentation Pack	.. ..	3·75		☐	
		PHQ Cards (set of 5)	..	2·75	4·50	☐	☐
		Set of 5 Gutter Pairs	..	6·00		☐	

Collectors Pack 1984

1984 (20 Nov.) *Comprises Nos. 1236/71*

Collectors Pack	.. ..	..	45·00	☐

Post Office Yearbook·

1984 *Comprises Nos. 1236/71 in hardbound book with slip case.*

Yearbook	.. ..	·.	85·00	☐

747 "The Flying Scotsman"

748 "The Golden Arrow"

749 "The Cheltenham Flyer"

750 "The Royal Scot"

751 "The Cornish Riviera"

754 Wart-Biter Bush-Cricket

755 Stag Beetle

756 Emperor Dragonfly

Famous Trains

1985 (22 Jan.) *Phosphorised paper*

1272	747	17p multicoloured	..	60	60	☐ ☐
1273	748	22p multicoloured	..	80	80	☐ ☐
1274	749	29p multicoloured	..	1·10	1·10	☐ ☐
1275	750	31p multicoloured	..	1·10	1·10	☐ ☐
1276	751	34p multicoloured	..	1·40	1·40	☐ ☐
		Set of 5		4·50	4·50	☐ ☐
		First Day Cover			7·00	☐
		Presentation Pack			6·00	☐
		PHQ Cards (set of 5) ..		3·50	11·00	☐ ☐
		Set of 5 Gutter Pairs		9·00		☐

Nos. 1272/6 were issued on the occasion of the 150th anniversary of the Great Western Railway Company.

Insects

1985 (12 March) *Phosphorised paper*

1277	752	17p multicoloured	..	50	55	☐ ☐
1278	753	22p multicoloured	..	70	70	☐ ☐
1279	754	29p multicoloured	..	90	90	☐ ☐
1280	755	31p multicoloured	..	1·10	1·10	☐ ☐
1281	756	34p multicoloured	..	1·10	1·10	☐ ☐
		Set of 5		4·00	4·00	☐ ☐
		First Day Cover			4·25	☐
		Presentation Pack			4·75	☐
		PHQ Cards (set of 5)		3·00	5·50	☐ ☐
		Set of 5 Gutter Pairs		8·00		☐

Nos. 1277/81 were issued on the occasion of the centenaries of the Royal Entomological Society of London's Royal Charter and of the Selborne Society.

752 Buff Tailed Bumble Bee

753 Seven Spotted Ladybird

757 "Water Music", by Handel

758 "The Planets", by Holst

759 "The First Cuckoo", by Delius

760 "Sea Pictures", by Elgar

Europa – European Music Year

1985 (14 May) *Phosphorised paper. Perf* 14½

1282	**757**	17p multicoloured	..	60	60	☐ ☐
1283	**758**	22p multicoloured	..	90	90	☐ ☐
1284	**759**	31p multicoloured	..	1·25	1·25	☐ ☐
1285	**760**	34p multicoloured	..	1·40	1·40	☐ ☐
		Set of 4		3·75	3·75	☐ ☐
		First Day Cover			4·00	☐
		Presentation Pack		4·25		☐
		PHQ Cards (set of 4) ..		2·50	5·25	☐ ☐
		Set of 4 Gutter Pairs		7·50		☐

Nos. 1282/5 were issued on the occasion of the 300th birth anniversary of Handel.

761 R.N.L.I. Lifeboat and Signal Flags

762 Beachy Head Lighthouse and Chart

763 "Marecs A" Communications Satellite and Dish Aerials

764 Buoys

Safety at Sea

1985 (18 June) *Phosphorised paper. Perf* 14

1286	**761**	17p multicoloured	..	50	50	☐ ☐
1287	**762**	22p multicoloured	..	75	75	☐ ☐
1288	**763**	31p multicoloured	..	1·10	1·10	☐ ☐
1289	**764**	34p multicoloured	..	1·25	1·25	☐ ☐
		Set of 4		3·25	3·25	☐ ☐
		First Day Cover			4·00	☐
		Presentation Pack		3·75		☐
		PHQ Cards (set of 4) ..		2·50	5·25	☐ ☐
		Set of 4 Gutter Pairs ..		6·50		☐

Nos. 1286/9 were issued on the occasion of the bicentenary of the unimmersible lifeboat and the 50th anniversary of Radar.

765 Datapost Motorcyclist, City of London

766 Rural Postbus

767 Parcel Delivery in Winter

768 Town Letter Delivery

350 Years of Royal Mail Public Postal Service

1985 (30 July) *Phosphorised paper*

1290	**765**	17p multicoloured	..	50	50	☐ ☐
1291	**766**	22p multicoloured	..	75	75	☐ ☐
1292	**767**	31p multicoloured	..	1·10	1·10	☐ ☐
1293	**768**	34p multicoloured	..	1·25	1·25	☐ ☐
		Set of 4		3·25	3·25	☐ ☐
		First Day Cover			3·75	☐
		Presentation Pack		3·75		☐
		PHQ Cards (set of 4) ..		2·50	5·25	☐ ☐
		Set of 4 Gutter Pairs ..		6·50		☐

769 King Arthur and Merlin

770 The Lady of the Lake

771 Queen Guinevere and
Sir Lancelot

772 Sir Galahad

777 Alfred Hitchcock (from
photo by Howard Coster)

Arthurian Legends

1985 (3 SEPT.) *Phosphorised paper*

1294	769	17p multicoloured	..	50	50	☐	☐
1295	770	22p multicoloured	..	75	75	☐	☐
1296	771	31p multicoloured	..	1·10	1·10	☐	☐
1297	772	34p multicoloured	..	1·25	1·25	☐	☐
		Set of 4	..	3·25	3·25	☐	☐
		First Day Cover	..		4·00		☐
		Presentation Pack ..	..	4·00		☐	
		PHQ Cards (set of 4)	..	2·50	5·25	☐	☐
		Set of 4 Gutter Pairs	..	6·50		☐	

Nos. 1294/7 were issued on the occasion of the 500th
anniversary of the printing of Sir Thomas Malory's *Morte
d'Arthur*.

British Film Year

1985 (8 OCT.) *Phosphorised paper. Perf 14½*

1298	773	17p multicoloured	..	40	40	☐	☐
1299	774	22p multicoloured	..	70	80	☐	☐
1300	775	29p multicoloured	..	1·10	90	☐	☐
1301	776	31p multicoloured	..	1·10	1·10	☐	☐
1302	777	34p multicoloured	..	1·10	1·10	☐	☐
		Set of 5	..	4·00	4·00	☐	☐
		First Day Cover	.. ..		5·00		☐
		Presentation Pack	.. ..	4·75		☐	
		Souvenir Book	.. ..	7·00		☐	
		PHQ Cards (set of 5)	..	2·75	5·75	☐	☐
		Set of 5 Gutter Pairs	..	8·00		☐	

778 Principal Boy

779 Genie

773 Peter Sellers (from photo
by Bill Brandt)

774 David Niven (from photo
by Cornell Lucas)

780 Dame

781 Good Fairy

775 Charlie Chaplin (from photo
by Lord Snowdon)

776 Vivien Leigh (from photo
by Angus McBean)

782 Pantomime Cat

Christmas. Pantomime Characters

1985 (19 Nov.) *One phosphor band* (12p) *or phosphorised paper (others)*

1303	778	12p multicoloured	..	35	35	☐	☐
1304	779	17p multicoloured	..	45	50	☐	☐
1305	780	22p multicoloured	..	75	75	☐	☐
1306	781	31p multicoloured	..	1·00	1·00	☐	☐
1307	782	34p multicoloured	..	1·10	1·10	☐	☐
		Set of 5	.. .. ..	3·25	3·25	☐	☐
		First Day Cover	.. ..		3·75		☐
		Presentation Pack	.. .. ..	4·00		☐	
		PHQ Cards (Set of 5)	.. ..	2·75	5·50	☐	☐
		Set of 5 Gutter Pairs	.. ..	6·50		☐	

Collectors Pack 1985

1985 (19 Nov.) *Comprises Nos.* 1272/1307

	Collectors Pack	.. .. ..	45·00		☐	

Post Office Yearbook

1985 *Comprises Nos.* 1272/1307 *in hardbound book with slip case.*

	Yearbook	.. ..	85·00		☐	

783 Light Bulb and North Sea Oil Drilling Rig (Energy)

784 Thermometer and Pharmaceutical Laboratory (Health)

785 Garden Hoe and Steel Works (Steel)

786 Loaf of Bread and Cornfield (Agriculture)

Industry Year

1986 (14 Jan.) *Phosphorised paper. Perf* $14\frac{1}{2} \times 14$

1308	783	17p multicoloured	..	45	45	☐	☐
1309	784	22p multicoloured	..	70	70	☐	☐
1310	785	31p multicoloured	..	1·10	1·10	☐	☐
1311	786	34p multicoloured	..	1·10	1·10	☐	☐
		Set of 4	.. .. ..	3·00	3·00	☐	☐
		First Day Cover	.. ..		4·50		☐
		Presentation Pack	.. ..	3·50		☐	
		PHQ Cards (set of 4)	.. ..	2·25	5·50	☐	☐
		Set of 4 Gutter Pairs	.. ..	6·00		☐	

787 Dr. Edmond Halley as Comet

788 *Giotto* Spacecraft approaching Comet

789 "Twice in a Lifetime"

790 Comet orbiting Sun and Planets

Appearance of Halley's Comet

1986 (18 Feb.) *Phosphorised paper.*

1312	787	17p multicoloured	..	45	45	☐	☐
1313	788	22p multicoloured	..	90	90	☐	☐
1314	789	31p multicoloured	..	1·25	1·25	☐	☐
1315	790	34p multicoloured	..	1·25	1·25	☐	☐
		Set of 4	.. ..	3·50	3·50	☐	☐
		First Day Cover	.. ..		5·00		☐
		Presentation Pack	.. ..	4·00		☐	
		PHQ Cards (set of 4)	.. ..	2·50	5·25	☐	☐
		Set of 4 Gutter Pairs	.. ..	7·00		☐	

791 Queen Elizabeth II in 1928, 1942 and 1952

792 Queen Elizabeth II in 1958, 1973 and 1982

Nos. 1316/17 and 1318/19 were each printed together, *se-tenant*, in horizontal pairs throughout the sheets.

60th Birthday of Queen Elizabeth II

1986 (21 Apr.) *Phosphorised paper.*

1316	791	17p multicoloured	..	60	60	☐	☐
		a. Horiz pair.					
		Nos.1316/17	..	1·60	1·60	☐	☐
1317	792	17p multicoloured	..	60	60	☐	☐
1318	791	34p multicoloured	..	1·10	1·10	☐	☐
		a. Horiz pair.					
		Nos.1318/19	..	2·50	2·50	☐	☐
1319	792	34p multicoloured	..	1·10	1·10	☐	☐
		Set of 4	.. ..	3·75	3·75	☐	☐
		First Day Cover	.. ..		4·50		☐
		Presentation Pack	.. ..	4·50		☐	
		Souvenir Book	.. ..	7·00		☐	
		PHQ Cards (set of 4)	.. ..	2·50	5·50	☐	☐
		Set of 4 Gutter Pairs	.. ..	7·50		☐	

793 Barn Owl

794 Pine Marten

795 Wild Cat

796 Natterjack Toad

Europa. Nature Conservation. Endangered Species

1986 (20 MAY) *Phosphorised paper. Perf 14½ × 14*

1320	**793**	17p multicoloured	..	50	55	☐	☐
1321	**794**	22p multicoloured	..	90	80	☐	☐
1322	**795**	31p multicoloured	..	1·25	1·25	☐	☐
1323	**796**	34p multicoloured	..	1·25	1·25	☐	☐
		Set of 4	.. ..	3·50	3·50	☐	☐
		First Day Cover	.. ..		4·50		☐
		Presentation Pack	.. ..	4·50		☐	
		PHQ Cards (set of 4)	..	2·00	5·25	☐	☐
		Set of 4 Gutter Pairs	.. ..	7·00		☐	

797 Peasants working in Fields

798 Freemen working at Town Trades

799 Knight and Retainers

800 Lord at Banquet

900th Anniversary of Domesday Book

1986 (17 JUNE) *Phosphorised paper*

1324	**797**	17p multicoloured	..	50	50	☐	☐
1325	**798**	22p multicoloured	..	90	90	☐	☐
1326	**799**	31p multicoloured	..	1·25	1·25	☐	☐
1327	**800**	34p multicoloured	..	1·25	1·25	☐	☐
		Set of 4	.. ..	3·50	3·50	☐	☐
		First Day Cover	.. ..		4·00		☐
		Presentation Pack	.. ..	4·50		☐	
		PHQ Cards (set of 4)	..	2·00	5·00	☐	☐
		Set of 4 Gutter Pairs	.. ..	7·00		☐	

801 Athletics

802 Rowing

803 Weightlifting

804 Rifle-Shooting

805 Hockey

Thirteenth Commonwealth Games, Edinburgh (Nos. 1328/31) and World Men's Hockey Cup, London (No. 1332)

1986 (15 JULY) *Phosphorised paper.*

1328	**801**	17p multicoloured	..	45	50	☐	☐
1329	**802**	22p multicoloured	..	90	60	☐	☐
1330	**803**	29p multicoloured	..	1·25	1·25	☐	☐
1331	**804**	31p multicoloured	..	1·25	1·25	☐	☐
1332	**805**	34p multicoloured	..	1·25	1·10	☐	☐
		Set of 5	.. ..	4·50	4·00	☐	☐
		First Day Cover	.. ..		5·50		☐
		Presentation Pack	.. ..	5·25		☐	
		PHQ Cards (Set of 5)	..	2·40	5·75	☐	☐
		Set of 5 Gutter Pairs	.. ..	9·00		☐	

No. 1332 also marked the centenary of the Hockey Association.

806 Prince Andrew and Miss Sarah Ferguson **807**

Royal Wedding

1986 (22 July) *One side band (12p) or phosphorised paper (17p)*

1333	**806**	12p multicoloured	..	60	60	☐	☐
1334	**807**	17p multicoloured	..	90	90	☐	☐
		Set of 2		1·50	1·50	☐	☐
		First Day Cover			·2·50	☐	
		Presentation Pack		2·00		☐	
		PHQ Cards (set of 2)		1·00	3·00	☐	☐
		Set of 2 Gutter Pairs		3·00		☐	

808 Stylised Cross on Ballot Paper

32nd Commonwealth Parliamentary Conference, London

1986 (19 Aug.) *Phosphorised paper. Perf 14 × 14½*

1335	**808**	34p multicoloured	..	1·50	1·50	☐	☐
		First Day Cover			2·00	☐	
		PHQ Card		50	1·75	☐	☐
		Gutter Pair		3·00		☐	

809 Lord Dowding and "Hurricane" **810** Lord Tedder and "Typhoon"

811 Lord Trenchard and "DH 9A" **812** Sir Arthur Harris and "Lancaster"

813 Lord Portal and "Mosquito"

History of the Royal Air Force

1986 (16th Sept.) *Phosphorised paper. Perf 14½ × 14.*

1336	**809**	17p multicoloured	..	40	40	☐	☐
1337	**810**	22p multicoloured	..	90	90	☐	☐
1338	**811**	29p multicoloured	..	1·10	1·10	☐	☐
1339	**812**	31p multicoloured	..	1·25	1·25	☐	☐
1340	**813**	34p multicoloured	..	1·25	1·25	☐	☐
		Set of 5		4·50	4·50	☐	☐
		First Day Cover			5·25	☐	
		Presentation Pack		5·25		☐	
		PHQ Cards (set of 5)		2·50	5·75	☐	☐
		Set of 5 Gutter Pairs		9·00		☐	

Nos. 1336/40 were issued to celebrate the 50th anniversary of the first R.A.F. Commands.

814 The Glastonbury Thorn **815** The Tanad Valley Plygain

816 The Hebrides Tribute **817** The Dewsbury Church Knell

818 The Hereford Boy Bishop

Christmas. Folk Customs

1986 One phosphor band (12p, 13p) or phosphorised paper (others)

1341	814	12p mult. (2 Dec.)	..	75	75 □ □	
1342		13p mult. (18 Nov.)	..	40	40 □ □	
1343	815	18p mult. (18 Nov.)	..	55	55 □ □	
1344	816	22p mult. (18 Nov.)	..	75	75 □ □	
1345	817	31p mult. (18 Nov.)	..	1·00	1·00 □ □	
1346	818	34p mult. (18 Nov.)	..	1·00	1·00 □ □	
		Set of 6 ..	.. .. ..	4·00	4·00 □ □	
		First Day Covers (2)			5·00 □	
		Presentation Pack (Nos. 1342/6)		4·50	□	
		PHQ Cards (set of 5) (Nos. 1342/6)		2·50	5·50 □ □	
		Set of 6 Gutter Pairs	..	8·00	□	

Collectors Pack 1986

1986 (18 Nov.) Comprises Nos. 1308/40, 1342/6.

Collectors Pack .. .. .. 40·00 □

Post Office Yearbook

1986 Comprises Nos. 1308/40, 1342/6 in hardbound book with slip case.

Yearbook .. .. .. 85·00 □

819 North American Blanket Flower

820 Globe Thistle

821 Echeveria

822 Autumn Crocus

Flower Photographs by Alfred Lammer

1987 (20 Jan.) Phosphorised paper. Perf $14\frac{1}{2} \times 14$

1347	819	18p multicoloured	..	50	50 □ □	
1348	820	22p multicoloured	..	80	80 □ □	
1349	821	31p multicoloured	..	1·10	1·10 □ □	
1350	822	34p multicoloured	..	1·25	1·25 □ □	
		Set of 4	..	3·25	3·25 □ □	
		First Day Cover ..	.. ..		4·00 □	
		Presentation Pack..	..	4·00	□	
		PHQ Cards (set of 4)	..	2·00	5·75 □ □	
		Set of 4 Gutter Pairs	..	6·50	□	

823 The Principia Mathematica

824 Motion of Bodies in Ellipses

825 Optick Treatise

826 The System of the World

300th Anniversary of The Principia Mathematica by Sir Isaac Newton

1987 (24 Mar.) Phosphorised paper.

1351	823	18p multicoloured	..	50	50 □ □	
1352	824	22p multicoloured	..	80	80 □ □	
1353	825	31p multicoloured	..	1·10	1·10 □ □	
1354	826	34p multicoloured	..	1·25	1·25 □ □	
		Set of 4	..	3·25	3·25 □ □	
		First Day Cover ..	..		4·00 □	
		Presentation Pack..	..	4·00	□	
		PHQ Cards (set of 4)	..	2·00	5·00 □ □	
		Set of 4 Gutter Pairs	..	6·50	□	

For full information on all future British issues, collectors should write to the British Post Office Philatelic Bureau, 20 Brandon Street, Edinburgh EH3 5TT

827 Willis Faber and Dumas Building, Ipswich

828 Pompidou Centre, Paris

829 Staatsgalerie, Stuttgart

830 European Investment Bank, Luxembourg

Europa. British Architects in Europe

1987 (12 MAY) *Phosphorised paper.*

1355	**827**	18p multicoloured	..	50	50	☐	☐
1356	**828**	22p multicoloured	..	80	80	☐	☐
1357	**829**	31p multicoloured	..	1·10	1·10	☐	☐
1358	**830**	34p multicoloured	..	1·25	1·25	☐	☐
		Set of 4	.. .. ..	3·25	3·25	☐	☐
		First Day Cover	.. .. ..		4·00		☐
		Presentation Pack ..		4·00		☐	
		PHQ Cards (set of 4)	..	2·00	5·00	☐	☐
		Set of 4 Gutter Pairs	.. ..	6·50		☐	

831 Brigade Members with Ashford Litter, 1887

832 Bandaging Blitz Victim, 1940

833 Volunteer with fainting Girl, 1965

834 Transport of Transplant Organ by Air Wing, 1987

Centenary of St. John Ambulance Brigade

1987 (16 JUNE) *Phosphorised paper. Perf 14 × 14½*

1359	**831**	18p multicoloured	..	50	50	☐	☐
1360	**832**	22p multicoloured	..	80	80	☐	☐
1361	**833**	31p multicoloured	..	1·10	1·10	☐	☐
1362	**834**	34p multicoloured	..	1·25	1·25	☐	☐
		Set of 4	.. .. ..	3·25	3·25	☐	☐
		First Day Cover	.. .. ..		4·00		☐
		Presentation Pack ..		4·00		☐	
		PHQ Cards (set of 4)	.. ..	2·00	5·00	☐	☐
		Set of 4 Gutter Pairs	.. ..	6·50		☐	

835 Arms of the Lord Lyon King of Arms

836 Scottish Heraldic Banner of Prince Charles

837 Arms of Royal Scottish Academy of Painting, Sculpture and Architecture

838 Arms of Royal Society of Edinburgh

300th Anniversary of Revival of Order of the Thistle

1987 (21 JULY) *Phosphorised paper. Perf 14½*

1363	**835**	18p multicoloured	..	50	50	☐	☐
1364	**836**	22p multicoloured	..	80	80	☐	☐
1365	**837**	31p multicoloured	..	1·10	1·10	☐	☐
1366	**838**	34p multicoloured	..	1·25	1·25	☐	☐
		Set of 4	.. .. ..	3·25	3·25	☐	☐
		First Day Cover	.. .. ..		4·00		☐
		Presentation Pack ..		4·00		☐	
		PHQ Cards (set of 4)	.. ..	2·00	5·00	☐	☐
		Set of 4 Gutter Pairs	.. ..	6·50		☐	

839 Crystal Palace, 'Monarch of the Glen' (Landseer) and Grace Darling

840 Great Eastern, Beeton's Book of Household Management and Prince Albert

841 Albert Memorial, Ballot Box and Disraeli

842 Diamond Jubilee Emblem, Morse Key and Newspaper Placard for Relief of Mafeking

150th Anniversary of Queen Victoria's Accession

1987 (8 Sept.) *Phosphorised paper.*

1367	**839**	18p multicoloured	..	50	50	☐	☐
1368	**840**	22p multicoloured	..	80	80	☐	☐
1369	**841**	31p multicoloured	..	1·10	1·10	☐	☐
1370	**842**	34p multicoloured	..	1·25	1·25	☐	☐
		Set of 4	.. .. ..	3·25	3·25	☐	☐
		First Day Cover	.. ..		4·00		☐
		Presentation Pack	..	4·00			☐
		PHQ Cards (set of 4)	..	2·00	5·00	☐	☐
		Set of 4 Gutter Pairs	.. ..	6·50			☐

843 Pot by Bernard Leach

844 Pot by Elizabeth Fritsch

845 Pot by Lucie Rie

846 Pot by Hans Coper

Studio Pottery

1987 (13 Oct.) *Phosphorised paper. Perf 14½ × 14*

1371	**843**	18p multicoloured	..	50	50	☐	☐
1372	**844**	26p multicoloured	..	80	80	☐	☐
1373	**845**	31p multicoloured	..	1·10	1·10	☐	☐
1374	**846**	34p multicoloured	..	1·25	1·25	☐	☐
		Set of 4	.. .. ..	3·25	3·25	☐	☐
		First Day Cover	.. ..		4·00		☐
		Presentation Pack	..	4·00			☐
		PHQ Cards (set of 4)	..	2·00	5·00	☐	☐
		Set of 4 Gutter Pairs		6·50			☐

Nos. 1371/4 also mark the birth centenary of Bernard Leach, the potter.

847 Decorating the Christmas tree

848 Waiting for Father Christmas

849 Sleeping Child and Father Christmas in Sleigh

850 Child reading

851 Child playing Flute and Snowman

Christmas

1987 (17 Nov.) *One phosphor band (13p) or phosphorised paper (others)*

1375	**847**	13p multicoloured	..	40	40	☐	☐
1376	**848**	18p multicoloured	..	50	50	☐	☐
1377	**849**	26p multicoloured	..	75	75	☐	☐
1378	**850**	31p multicoloured	..	90	90	☐	☐
1379	**851**	34p multicoloured	..	1·00	1·00	☐	☐
		Set of 5	.. .. ..	3·25	3·25	☐	☐
		First Day Cover	.. ..		4·00		☐
		Presentation Pack	..	3·75			☐
		PHQ Cards (set of 5)	..	2·25	5·75	☐	☐
		Set of 5 Gutter Pairs	.. ..	6·50			☐

Collectors Pack 1987

1987 (17 Nov.) *Comprises Nos.* 1347/79
 Collectors Pack .. .. .. 30·00 ☐

Post Office Yearbook

1987 *Comprises Nos.* 1347/79 *in hardbound book with slip case*
 Yearbook .. .. 60·00 ☐

852 Bull-rout (Jonathan Couch)

853 Yellow Waterlily (Major Joshua Swatkin)

854 Bewick's Swan (Edward Lear)

855 *Morchella esculenta* (James Sowerby)

Bicentenary of Linnean Society. Archive Illustrations

1988 (19 Jan.) *Phosphorised paper*

1380	**852**	18p multicoloured ..	45	45	☐ ☐
1381	**853**	26p multicoloured	75	75	☐ ☐
1382	**854**	31p multicoloured	1·00	1·00	☐ ☐
1383	**855**	34p multicoloured	1·10	1·10	☐ ☐
		Set of 4	3·00	3·00	☐ ☐
		First Day Cover		3·75	☐
		Presentation Pack	3·75		☐
		PHQ Cards (set of 4) ..	2·00	5·00	☐ ☐
		Set of 4 Gutter Pairs ..	6·00		☐

856 Revd William Morgan (Bible translator, 1588)

857 William Salesbury (New Testament translator, 1567)

858 Bishop Richard Davies (New Testament translator, 1567)

859 Bishop Richard Parry (editor of Revised Welsh Bible, 1620)

400th Anniversary of Welsh Bible

1988 (1 Mar.) *Phosphorised paper. Perf* 14½ × 14

1384	**856**	18p multicoloured ..	45	45	☐ ☐
1385	**857**	26p multicoloured	75	75	☐ ☐
1386	**858**	31p multicoloured	1·00	1·00	☐ ☐
1387	**859**	34p multicoloured	1·10	1·10	☐ ☐
		Set of 4	3·00	3·00	☐ ☐
		First Day Cover		3·75	☐
		Presentation Pack ..	3·75		☐
		PHQ Cards (set of 4) ..	2·00	5·00	☐ ☐
		Set of 4 Gutter Pairs ..	6·00		☐

860 Gymnastics (Centenary of British Amateur Gymnastics Association)

861 Downhill Skiing (Ski Club of Great Britain)

862 Tennis (Centenary of Lawn Tennis Association)

863 Football (Centenary of Football League)

Sports Organizations

1988 (22 MAR.) *Phosphorised paper. Perf* 14½

1388	**860**	18p multicoloured	..	45	45	☐ ☐
1389	**861**	26p multicoloured		75	75	☐ ☐
1390	**862**	31p multicoloured		1·00	1·00	☐ ☐
1391	**863**	34p multicoloured		1·10	1·10	☐ ☐
		Set of 4		3·00	3·00	☐ ☐
		First Day Cover			6·00	☐
		Presentation Pack		3·75		☐
		PHQ Cards (set of 4)		2·00	5·00	☐ ☐
		Set of 4 Gutter Pairs		6·00		☐

864 *Mallard* and Mailbags on Pick-up Arms

865 Loading Transatlantic Mail on Liner *Queen Elizabeth*

866 Glasgow Tram No. 1173 and Pillar Box

867 Imperial Airways Handley Page "HP 24" and Airmail Van

Europa. Transport and Mail Services in 1930's

1988 (10 MAY) *Phosphorised paper*

1392	**864**	18p multicoloured	..	50	50	☐ ☐
1393	**865**	26p multicoloured	..	70	70	☐ ☐
1394	**866**	31p multicoloured	..	1·00	1·00	☐ ☐
1395	**867**	34p multicoloured	..	1·10	1·10	☐ ☐
		Set of 4		3·00	3·00	☐ ☐
		First Day Cover			3·75	☐
		Presentation Pack		3·75		☐
		PHQ Cards (set of 4)		2·00	5·00	☐ ☐
		Set of 4 Gutter Pairs		6·00		☐

868 Early Settler and Sailing Clipper

869 Queen Elizabeth II with British and Australian Parliament Buildings

870 W. G. Grace (cricketer) and Tennis Racquet

871 Shakespeare, John Lennon (entertainer) and Sydney Landmarks

Nos. 1396/7 and 1398/9 were each printed together, *se-tenant*, in horizontal pairs throughout the sheets, each pair showing a background design of the Australian flag.

Bicentenary of Australian Settlement

1988 (21 JUNE) *Phosphorised paper. Perf* 14½

1396	**868**	18p multicoloured	..	50	35	☐ ☐
		a. Horiz. pair.				
		Nos. 1396/7 ..	..	1·10	1·10	☐ ☐
1397	**869**	18p multicoloured	..	50	35	☐ ☐
1398	**870**	34p multicoloured	..	1·10	1·00	☐ ☐
		a. Horiz. pair.				
		Nos. 1398/9 ..	..	2·25	2·25	☐ ☐
1399	**871**	34p multicoloured	..	1·10	1·10	☐ ☐
		Set of 4		3·00	3·00	☐ ☐
		First Day Cover			4·00	☐
		Presentation Pack		3·50		☐
		Souvenir Book		6·00		☐
		PHQ Cards (set of 4)		2·00	5·00	☐ ☐
		Set of 4 Gutter Pairs		6·00		☐

Stamps in similar designs were also issued by Australia.

872 Spanish Galeasse off The Lizard

873 English Fleet leaving Plymouth

874 Engagement off Isle of Wight

875 Attack of English Fire-ships, Calais

876 Armada in Storm,
North Sea

Nos. 1400/4 were printed together, *se-tenant*, in horizontal strips of 5 throughout the sheet, forming a composite design.

400th Anniversary of Spanish Armada

1988 (19 JULY) *Phosphorised paper*

1400	**872**	18p multicoloured	..	65	65	☐	☐
		a. Horiz strip of 5.					
		Nos. 1400/4 ..	..	2·75	2·75	☐	☐
1401	**873**	18p multicoloured	..	65	65	☐	☐
1402	**874**	18p multicoloured	..	65	65	☐	☐
1403	**875**	18p multicoloured	..	65	65	☐	☐
1404	**876**	18p multicoloured	..	65	65	☐	☐
		Set of 5	.. ..	2·75	2·75	☐	☐
		First Day Cover ..	.. ..		3·50		☐
		Presentation Pack ..	.. ..	3·25		☐	
		PHQ Cards (set of 5)	.. ..	2·00	4·75	☐	☐
		Gutter strip of 10	.. ..	5·50		☐	

877 "The Owl and the
Pussy-cat"

878 "Edward Lear as a Bird"
(self-portrait)

879 "Cat" (from alphabet
book)

880 "There was a Young Lady
whose Bonnet . . ."
(limerick)

Death Centenary of Edward Lear (artist and author)

1988 (6–27 SEPT.) *Phosphorised paper*

1405	**877**	19p black, pale cream and carmine	50	50	☐	☐
1406	**878**	27p black, pale cream and yellow	80	80	☐	☐
1407	**879**	32p black, pale cream and emerald	1·00	1·00	☐	☐
1408	**880**	35p black, pale cream and blue ..	1·10	1·10	☐	☐
		Set of 4	3·00	3·00	☐	☐
		First Day Cover		3·75		☐
		Presentation Pack	3·50		☐	
		PHQ Cards (set of 4)	2·00	5·00	☐	☐
		Set of 4 Gutter Pairs	6·00		☐	
MS1409		122×90 mm. Nos. 1405/8	7·50	7·00	☐	☐
		First Day Cover (27 Sept.) ..		7·50		☐

No. **MS**1409 was sold at £1·35, the premium being used for the "Stamp World London 90" International Stamp Exhibition.

881 Carrickfergus Castle

882 Caernarvon Castle

883 Edinburgh Castle

884 Windsor Castle

1988 (18 OCT.) *Ordinary paper*

1410	**881**	£1 deep green	.. ..	1·50	1·60	☐	☐
1411	**882**	£1·50 maroon	.. ..	2·25	2·40	☐	☐
1412	**883**	£2 steel blue	.. ..	3·00	3·25	☐	☐
1413	**884**	£5 deep brown	.. ..	7·50	7·75	☐	☐
		Set of 4	.. ..	13·00	13·50	☐	☐
		First Day Cover	..		40·00		☐
		Presentation Pack		14·00		☐	
		Set of 4 Gutter Pairs		27·00		☐	

885 Journey to Bethlehem

886 Shepherds and Star

887 Three Wise Men

888 Nativity

889 The Annunciation

890 Puffin

891 Avocet

892 Oystercatcher

893 Gannet

Christmas

1988 (15 Nov.) *One phosphor band* (14p) *or phosphorised paper* (*others*)

1414	**885**	14p multicoloured	..	35	35	☐	☐
1415	**886**	19p multicoloured	..	50	50	☐	☐
1416	**887**	27p multicoloured	..	80	80	☐	☐
1417	**888**	32p multicoloured	..	1·00	1·00	☐	☐
1418	**889**	35p multicoloured	..	1·00	1·00	☐	☐
		Set of 5		3·25	3·25	☐	☐
		First Day Cover			4·00		☐
		Presentation Pack ..		3·75		☐	
		PHQ Cards (set of 5)		2·00	5·25	☐	☐
		Set of 5 Gutter Pairs		· 6·50		☐	

Collectors Pack 1988

1988 (15 Nov.) *Comprises Nos.* 1380/1408, 1414/18

	Collectors Pack		25·00	☐

Post Office Yearbook

1988 *Comprises Nos.* 1380/1404. **MS**1409, 1414/18 *in hardbound book with slip case*

	Yearbook		45·00	☐

Centenary of Royal Society for the Protection of Birds

1989 (17 Jan.) *Phosphorised paper*

1419	**890**	19p multicoloured	..	50	50	☐	☐
1420	**891**	27p multicoloured	..	75	75	☐	☐
1421	**892**	32p multicoloured	..	90	90	☐	☐
1422	**893**	35p multicoloured	..	90	90	☐	☐
		Set of 4		2·75	2·75	☐	☐
		First Day Cover			4·00		☐
		Presentation Pack		3·00		☐	
		PHQ Cards (set of 4)		2·00	4·50	☐	☐
		Set of 4 Gutter Pairs		5·50		☐	

894 Rose

895 Cupid

896 Yachts

897 Fruit

898 Teddy Bear

Nos. 1423/7 were printed together, *se-tenant*, in horizontal strips of five, two such strips forming the booklet pane.

Greetings Booklet Stamps

1989 (31 JAN.) *Phosphorised paper*

1423	**894**	19p multicoloured	..	1·50	1·50	☐ ☐
		a. *Booklet pane.*				
		Nos. 1423/7 × 2	..	15·00		☐
1424	**895**	19p multicoloured	..	1·50	1·50	☐ ☐
1425	**896**	19p multicoloured	..	1·50	1·50	☐ ☐
1426	**897**	19p multicoloured	..	1·50	1·50	☐ ☐
1427	**898**	19p multicoloured	..	1·50	1·50	☐ ☐
		Set of 5	..	7·50	7·50	☐ ☐
		First Day Cover	..		8·00	☐

899 Fruit and Vegetables

900 Meat Products

901 Dairy Produce

902 Cereal Products

Food and Farming Year

1989 (7 MAR.) *Phosphorised paper. Perf* $14 \times 14\frac{1}{2}$

1428	**899**	19p multicoloured	..	50	50	☐ ☐
1429	**900**	27p multicoloured	..	75	75	☐ ☐
1430	**901**	32p multicoloured	..	90	90	☐ ☐
1431	**902**	35p multicoloured	..	90	90	☐ ☐
		Set of 4	..	2·75	2·75	☐ ☐
		First Day Cover	..		4·00	☐
		Presentation Pack		3·00		☐
		PHQ Cards (set of 4) ..	..	2·00	4·50	☐ ☐
		Set of 4 Gutter Pairs ..	..	5·50		☐

903 Mortar Board (150th Anniv of Public Education in England)

904 Cross on Ballot Paper (3rd Direct Elections to European Parliament)

905 Posthorn (26th Postal, Telegraph and Telephone International Congress Brighton)

906 Globe (Inter-Parliamentary Union Centenary Conference, London)

Nos. 1432/3 and 1434/5 were each printed together, *se-tenant*, in horizontal pairs throughout the sheets.

Anniversaries

1989 (11 APR.) *Phosphorised paper. Perf* $14 \times 14\frac{1}{2}$

1432	**903**	19p multicoloured	..	45	45	☐ ☐
		a. *Horiz pair.*				
		Nos. 1432/3	..	95	95	☐ ☐
1433	**904**	19p multicoloured	..	45	45	☐ ☐
1434	**905**	35p multicoloured	..	1·00	95	☐ ☐
		a. *Horiz pair.*				
		Nos. 1434/5	..	2·10	2·10	☐ ☐
1435	**906**	35p multicoloured	..	1·00	95	☐ ☐
		Set of 4	..	2·75	2·75	☐ ☐
		First Day Cover	..		4·00	☐
		Presentation Pack	..	3·00		☐
		PHQ Cards (set of 4) ..	..	2·00	4·50	☐ ☐
		Set of 2 Gutter Pairs ..	..	3·00		☐

907 Toy Train and Airplane

908 Building Bricks

909 Dice and Board Games   **910** Toy Robot, Boat and Doll's House

915

Industrial Archaeology

1989 (4–25 JULY) *Phosphorised paper*

1440	**911**	19p multicoloured	..	50	50	☐	☐
1441	**912**	27p multicoloured	..	75	75	☐	☐
1442	**913**	32p multicoloured	..	90	90	☐	☐
1443	**914**	35p multicoloured	..	90	90	☐	☐
		Set of 4	..	2·75	2·75	☐	☐
		First Day Cover	..		4·00		☐
		Presentation Pack	..	3·25		☐	
		PHQ Cards (set of 4) ..	..	90	4·50	☐	☐
		Set of 4 Gutter Pairs ..	..	5·75		☐	

MS1444   122 × 90 mm. **915** As Nos.
1440/3 but designs horizontal   ..   4·00   4·00 ☐ ☐
    First Day Cover (25 July)   ..   4·50 ☐

No.**MS**1444 was sold at £1.40, the premium being used for the "Stamp World London 90" International Stamp Exhibition.

Europa. Games and Toys

1989 (16 MAY) *Phosphorised paper*

1436	**907**	19p multicoloured	..	50	50	☐	☐
1437	**908**	27p multicoloured	..	75	75	☐	☐
1438	**909**	32p multicoloured	..	90	90	☐	☐
1439	**910**	35p multicoloured	..	90	90	☐	☐
		Set of 4	..	2·75	2·75	☐	☐
		First Day Cover	..		4·00		☐
		Presentation Pack	..	3·00		☐	
		PHQ Cards (set of 4) ..	..	2·00	4·50	☐	☐
		Set of 4 Gutter Pairs ..	..	5·50		☐	

916

917

911 Ironbridge, Shropshire

912 Tin Mine, St. Agnes Head, Cornwall

Booklet Stamps

1989 (22 AUG.) **– 90**

(a) Printed in photogravure by Harrison and Sons. Perf 15 × 14

1445	**916**	(2nd) bright blue (1 centre band)	45	45	☐	☐
1446		(2nd) bright blue (1 side band) (20.3.90) ..	45	45	☐	☐
1447	**917**	(1st) black (phosphorised paper)	75	75	☐	☐
1448		(1st) brownish black (2 bands) (20.3.90) ..	75	75	☐	☐

(b) Printed in lithography by Walsall. Perf 14

1449	**916**	(2nd) bright blue (1 centre band) ..	45	45	☐	☐
1450	**917**	(1st) black (2 bands) ..	75	75	☐	☐

913 Cotton Mills, New Lanark, Strathclyde

914 Pontcysyllte Aqueduct, Clwyd

(c) Printed in lithography by Questa. Perf 15 × 14

1451	**916**	(2nd) bright blue (1 centre band) (19.9.89) ..	45	45	☐	☐
1452	**917**	(1st) black (phosphorised paper) (19.9.89)	75	75	☐	☐

First Day Cover (Nos. 1445, 1447) .. .. .. 2·50 ☐

918 Snowflake (× 10)

919 Blue Fly (× 5)

920 Blood Cells (× 500)

921 Microchip (× 600)

150th Anniversary of Royal Microscopical Society

1989 (5 Sept.) *Phosphorised paper. Perf* 14½ × 14

1453	**918**	19p multicoloured	..	50	50	☐ ☐
1454	**919**	27p multicoloured	..	75	75	☐ ☐
1455	**920**	32p multicoloured	..	90	90	☐ ☐
1456	**921**	35p multicoloured	..	90	90	☐ ☐
	Set of 4			2·75	2·75	☐ ☐
	First Day Cover				4·00	☐
	Presentation Pack			3·00		☐
	PHQ Cards (set of 4)			2·00	4·50	☐ ☐
	Set of 4 Gutter Pairs			5·50		☐

922 Royal Mail Coach

923 Escort of Blues and Royals

924 Lord Mayor's Coach

925 Coach Team passing St Paul's

926 Blues and Royals Drum Horse

Nos. 1457/61 were printed together, *se-tenant*, in horizontal strips of 5 throughout the sheet, forming a composite design.

Lord Mayor's Show, London

1989 (17 Oct.) *Phosphorised paper*

1457	**922**	20p multicoloured	..	50	50	☐ ☐
		a. Horiz strip of 5. Nos. 1457/61 ..	2·25	2·25	☐ ☐
1458	**923**	20p multicoloured	..	50	50	☐ ☐
1459	**924**	20p multicoloured	..	50	50	☐ ☐
1460	**925**	20p multicoloured	..	50	50	☐ ☐
1461	**926**	20p multicoloured	..	50	50	☐ ☐
	Set of 5			2·25	2·25	☐ ☐
	First Day Cover				3·50	☐
	Presentation Pack			2·50		☐
	PHQ Cards (set of 5)			2·00	3·75	☐ ☐
	Gutter Strip of 10			4·50		☐

Nos. 1457/61 commemorate the 800th anniversary of the installation of the first Lord Mayor of London.

927 14th-century Peasants from Stained-glass Window

928 Arches and Roundels, West Front

929 Octagon Tower

930 Arcade from West Transept

931 Triple Arch from West Front

Christmas. 800th Anniversary of Ely Cathedral

1989 (14 Nov.) *One phosphor band (Nos. 1462/3) or phosphorised paper (others)*

1462	**927**	15p gold, silver and blue	35	35	□	□
1463	**928**	15p + 1p gold, silver and blue	40	40	□	□
1464	**929**	20p + 1p gold, silver and rosine	50	50	□	□
1465	**930**	34p + 1p gold, silver and emerald	85	85	□	□
1466	**931**	37p + 1p gold, silver and yellow-olive	1·00	1·00	□	□
		Set of 5	2·75	2·75	□	□
		First Day Cover		4·00		□
		Presentation Pack	3·00		□	
		PHQ Cards (set of 5)	2·00	4·25	□	
		Set of 5 Gutter Pairs	5·50		□	

Collectors Pack 1989

1989 (14 Nov.) *Comprises Nos.* 1419/22, 1428/43 *and* 1453/66

	Collectors Pack	25·00		□

Post Office Yearbook

1989 (14 Nov) *Comprises Nos.* 1419/22, 1428/44 *and* 1453/66 *in hardback book with slip case.*

	Yearbook	45·00		□

932 Queen Victoria and Queen Elizabeth II

150th Anniversary of the Penny Black

1990 (10 JAN.–17 APR.)

(a) Printed in photogravure by Harrison and Sons. Perf 15 × 14

1467	**932**	15p bright blue (1 centre band)	25	30	□	□
1468		15p bright blue (1 side band) (30 Jan) ..	25	30	□	□
1469		20p brownish black and cream (phosphorised paper)	30	35	□	□
1470		20p brnish blk & cream (2 bands) (30 Jan)	30	35	□	□
1471		29p deep mauve (phosphorised paper) ..	45	50	□	□
1472		29p deep mauve (2 bands) (20 Mar) ..	1·10	1·25	□	□
1473		34p deep bluish grey (phosphorised paper)	55	55	□	□
1474		37p rosine (phosphorised paper)	60	65	□	□
		Set of 5 (Nos. 1467, 1469, 1471, 1473/4)	2·00	2·25	□	□
		First Day Cover (Nos. 1467, 1469, 1471, 1473/4) ..		3·00		□
		Presentation Pack (Nos. 1467, 1469, 1471, 1473/4)	2·40		□	

(b) Litho Walsall. Perf 14 (30 Jan)

1475	**932**	15p bright blue (1 centre band) ..	25	30	□	□
1476		20p brnish blk & cream (phosphorised paper)	30	35	□	□
		Set of 2	55	65	□	□

(c) Litho Questa. Perf 15 × 14 (17 Apr)

1477	**932**	15p bright blue (1 centre band) ..	25	30	□	□
1478		20p brnish black (phosphorised paper) ..	30	35	□	□
		Set of 2	55	65	□	□

No. 1468 exists with the phosphor band at the left or right of the stamp.

933 Kitten

934 Rabbit

935 Duckling   **936** Puppy

150th Anniversary of Royal Society for Prevention of Cruelty to Animals

1990 (23 JAN.) *Phosphorised paper. Perf* $14 \times 14\frac{1}{2}$.

1479	**933**	20p multicoloured	..	30	35	□	□
1480	**934**	29p multicoloured	..	45	50	□	□
1481	**935**	34p multicoloured	..	55	60	□	□
1482	**936**	37p multicoloured	..	60	65	□	□
		Set of 4		1·75	1·90	□	□
		First Day Cover			3·00	□	
		Presentation Pack		2·25		□	
		PHQ Cards (set of 4)		1·10	4·75	□	□
		Set of 4 Gutter Pairs		3·75		□	

937 Teddy Bear   **938** Dennis the Menace

939 Punch   **940** Cheshire Cat

941 The Man in the Moon   **942** The Laughing Policeman

943 Clown   **944** Mona Lisa

945 Queen of Hearts   **946** Stan Laurel (comedian)

T **937**/46 were printed together, *se-tenant,* in booklet panes of 10.

Greetings Booklet Stamps. ''Smiles''

1990 (6 FEB.) *Two phosphor bands*

1483	**937**	20p multicoloured	..	30	35	□	□
		a. Booklet pane.					
		Nos. 1483/92	..	3·00		□	
1484	**938**	20p multicoloured	..	30	35	□	□
1485	**939**	20p multicoloured	..	30	35	□	□
1486	**940**	20p multicoloured	..	30	35	□	□
1487	**941**	20p multicoloured	..	30	35	□	□
1488	**942**	20p multicoloured	..	30	35	□	□
1489	**943**	20p multicoloured	..	30	35	□	□
1490	**944**	20p multicoloured	..	30	35	□	□
1491	**945**	20p multicoloured	..	30	35	□	□
1492	**946**	20p gold and grey-black		30	35	□	□
		Set of 10		3·00	3·50	□	□
		First Day Cover			4·50	□	

947 Alexandra Palace (''Stamp World London 90'' Exhibition)   **948** Glasgow School of Art

949 British Philatelic Bureau, Edinburgh

950 Templeton Carpet Factory, Glasgow

Europa (Nos. 1493 and 1495) and "Glasgow 1990 European City of Culture" (Nos. 1494 and 1496)

1990 (6 MAR.) *Phosphorised paper*

1493	**947**	20p multicoloured	..	30	35	☐ ☐
1494	**948**	20p multicoloured	..	30	35	☐ ☐
1495	**949**	29p multicoloured	..	45	50	☐ ☐
1496	**950**	37p multicoloured	..	60	65	☐ ☐
		Set of 4		1·50	1·60	☐ ☐
		First Day Cover			3·00	☐
		Presentation Pack		2·00		☐
		PHQ Cards (set of 4) ..		1·10	4·75	☐ ☐
		Set of 4 Gutter Pairs ..		3·25		☐

951 Export Achievement Award

952 Technological Achievement Award

Nos. 1497/8 and 1499/500 were each printed together, *se-tenant*, in horizontal pairs throughout the sheets.

25th Anniversary of Queen's Awards for Export and Technology

1990 (10 APR.) *Phosphorised paper. Perf* 14 × 14½.

1497	**951**	20p multicoloured	..	30	35	☐ ☐
		a. Horiz pair.				
		Nos. 1497/8 ..	..	60	70	☐ ☐
1498	**952**	20p multicoloured	..	30	35	☐ ☐
1499	**951**	37p multicoloured	..	60	65	☐ ☐
		a. Horiz pair.				
		Nos. 1499/500	..	1·25	1·25	☐ ☐
1500	**952**	37p multicoloured	..	60	65	☐ ☐
		Set of 4		1·60	1·75	☐ ☐
		First Day Cover			3·00	☐
		Presentation Pack ..	\..	2·00		☐
		PHQ Cards (set of 4) ..		1·10	4·75	☐ ☐
		Set of 2 Gutter Pairs ..		1·75		☐

953

"Stamp World 90" International Stamp Exhibition, London

1990 (3 MAY.) *Sheet* 122 × 90 *mm. Phosphorised paper*

MS1501	**953**	20p. brownish black				
	and cream	.. ..	1·50	1·75	☐ ☐
		First Day Cover	2·50		☐
		Souvenir Book (Nos. 1467,				
		1469, 1471, 1473/4 *and*				
		MS1501)	10·50		☐

No. **MS**1501 was sold at £1, the premium being used for the exhibition.

954 Cycad and Sir Joseph Banks Building

955 Stone Pine and Princess of Wales Conservatory

956 Willow Tree and Palm House

957 Cedar Tree and Pagoda

Stanley Gibbons STANDARD Great Britain Album

Based on the popular DAVO Great Britain standard album and therefore including all the following special features.

- ★ High Capacity
- ★ Superb Quality Materials
- ★ Handmade to the highest specifications
- ★ Attractive Cover design
- ★ Selected stamp illustrations
- ★ Professional layout
- ★ Luxury Slip case
- ★ Exceptional Value for Money

PLUS – we have added extra pages for the Machin definitives providing spaces for the popular phosphor band variations.

Because of its large page size and high capacity, it is able to house an entire Great Britain collection from 1840 to 1989 in a single volume and it therefore represents fantastic value for money when compared with other albums, some of which are already in three separate volumes.

POSITIVELY THE BEST VALUE GREAT BRITAIN ALBUM ON THE MARKET

Item 5284STSG

Stanley Gibbons Standard Great Britain Album 1840–1989

£25.00

Note: The 1990 supplement for the Stanley Gibbons Great Britain Standard Album (Item 5284ST90) will be published mid-December, price £5.50.

150th Anniversary of Kew Gardens

1990 (5 June) *Phosphorised paper*

1502	954	20p multicoloured	..	30	35	☐	☐
1503	955	29p multicoloured		45	50	☐	☐
1504	956	34p multicoloured		55	60	☐	☐
1505	957	37p multicoloured		60	65	☐	☐
		Set of 4		1·75	1·90	☐	☐
		First Day Cover			2·50		☐
		Presentation Pack		2·25			☐
		PHQ Cards (set of 4)		1·10	4·75	☐	☐
		Set of 4 Gutter Pairs		3·75			☐

958 Thomas Hardy and Clyffe Clump, Dorset

150th Birth Anniversary of Thomas Hardy (author)

1990 (10 July) *Phosphorised paper*

1506	958	20p multicoloured	..	30	35	☐	☐
		First Day Cover			85		☐
		Presentation Pack		70			☐
		PHQ Card		30	1·50	☐	☐
		Gutter Pair		65			☐

959 Queen Elizabeth the Queen Mother

960 Queen Elizabeth

961 Elizabeth, Duchess of York

962 Lady Elizabeth Bowes-Lyon

90th Birthday of Queen Elizabeth the Queen Mother

1990 (2 Aug.) *Phosphorised paper*

1507	959	20p multicoloured	..	30	35	☐	☐
1508	960	29p silver, indigo and grey-blue		45	50	☐	☐
1509	961	34p multicoloured		55	60	☐	☐
1510	962	37p silver, sepia and stone		60	65	☐	☐
		Set of 4		1·75	1·90	☐	☐
		First Day Cover			2·50		☐
		Presentation Pack		2·25			☐
		PHQ Cards (set of 4)		1·10	4·75	☐	☐
		Set of 4 Gutter Pairs		3·75			☐

Booklet Stamps

1990 (7 Aug.) *As Types* **916/17**, *but colours changed*

(a) Photo Harrison, Perf 15 × 14

1511	916	(2nd) dp blue (1 centre band) ..		25	30	☐	☐
1512	917	(1st) brt orge-red (phosphorised paper)		30	35	☐	☐

(a) Litho Questa. Perf 15 × 14

1513	916	(2nd) dp blue (1 centre band) ..		25	30	☐	☐
1514	917	(1st) brt orge-red (phosphorised paper)		30	35	☐	☐

(c) Litho Walsall. Perf 14

1515	916	(2nd) dp blue (1 centre band)		25	30	☐	☐
1516	917	(1st) brt orge-red (phosphorised paper)		30	35	☐	☐
		First Day Cover (Nos. 1515/16)			1·10		☐

963 Victoria Cross

964 George Cross

965 Distinguished Service Cross and Distinguished Service Medal

966 Military Cross and Military Medal

967 Distinguished Flying Cross and Distinguished Flying Medal

Gallantry Awards

1990 (11 SEPT.) *Phosphorised paper*

1517	**963**	20p multicoloured	..	30	35	□	□
1518	**964**	20p multicoloured	..	30	35	□	□
1519	**965**	20p multicoloured	..	30	35	□	□
1520	**966**	20p multicoloured	..	30	35	□	□
1521	**967**	20p multicoloured	..	30	35	□	□
		Set of 5	..	1·40	1·60	□	□
		First Day Cover			2·25	□	
		Presentation Pack		1·90		□	
		PHQ Cards (set of 5)	.. ..	1·40	4·25	□	□
		Set of 5 *Gutter Pairs*	.. ..	3·00		□	

968 Armagh Observatory, Jodrell Bank Radio Telescope and La Palma Telescope

969 Newton's Moon and Tides Diagram with Early Telescopes

970 Greenwich Old Observatory and Early Astronomical Equipment

971 Stonehenge, Gyroscope and Navigating by Stars

Astronomy

1990 (16 OCT.) *Phosphorised paper. Perf* 14 × 14½

1522	**968**	22p multicoloured	..	35	40	□	□
1523	**969**	26p multicoloured	..	40	45	□	□
1524	**970**	31p multicoloured	..	50	55	□	□
1525	**971**	37p multicoloured	..	60	65	□	□
		Set of 4	..	1·60	1·90	□	□
		First Day Cover			2·40	□	
		Presentation Pack ..		2·25		□	
		PHQ Cards (Set of 4)	..	1·10	4·75	□	□
		Set of 4 *Gutter Pairs* .	.. ..	3·50		□	

Nos. 1522/5 commemorate the centenary of the British Astronomical Association and the bicentenary of the Armagh Observatory.

972 Building a Snowman

973 Fetching the Christmas Tree

974 Carol Singing

975 Tobogganing

976 Ice-skating

Christmas

1990 (13 NOV.) *One phosphor band* (17p) *or phosphorised paper (others)*

1526	**972**	17p multicoloured	..	30	35	□	□
1527	**973**	22p multicoloured	..	35	40	□	□
1528	**974**	26p multicoloured	..	40	45	□	□
1529	**975**	31p multicoloured	..	50	55	□	□
1530	**976**	37p multicoloured	..	60	65	□	□
		Set of 5	..	1·90	2·10	□	□
		First Day Cover			2·50	□	
		Presentation Pack ..		2·25		□	
		PHQ Cards (Set of 5)	..	1·40	4·25	□	□
		Set of 5 *Gutter Pairs* .	.. ..	4·00		□	

Collectors Pack 1990

1990 (13 NOV.) *Comprises Nos.* 1479/82, 1493/1510 *and* 1517/30

Collectors Pack	.. ..	..	15·75	□

Post Office Yearbook

1990 *Comprises Nos.* 1479/82, 1493/500, 1502/10 *and* 1517/30 *in hardback book with slip case.*

Yearbook	.. ..	..	28·00	□

BY APPOINTMENT TO
HER MAJESTY THE QUEEN.
STANLEY GIBBONS LTD
PHILATELISTS

STANLEY GIBBONS LTD
GREAT BRITAIN
MAIL ORDER SERVICE

How can we help you improve your collection?

★ We offer you a fast, friendly and efficient service backed by a reputation built up over 134 years of dealing.

★ The range and depth of our stock is renowned world-wide. Most items we can supply to you immediately – always in the highest quality, and of course backed by the Stanley Gibbons guarantee of genuineness.

★ To help you fill your more expensive gaps we can offer an interest free payment system which spreads the cost for you over three months.

★ We can also offer you a Budget Plan which will allow you to add to your collection on a regular basis and at a monthly payment rate that you can afford.

★ Our regular Mail Order clients have the benefit of exclusive discounts and special offers not made available elsewhere.

For further details of how we can help you just contact Michael Barrell at the address below. If you would also like to order some items from our stock simply use the order form overleaf.

Michael Barrell, Great Britain (Mail Order) Service
399 Strand, London WC2R 0LX
Tel: 071-836 8444   Fax: 071-836 7342

STANLEY GIBBONS LTD
GREAT BRITAIN
MAIL ORDER SERVICE
ORDER FORM

To order simply fill out the form below (continuing on a separate sheet if necessary). Cut along the dotted line and send it with payment details to Michael Barrell at the address overleaf.

Please note that all items will be supplied at the prices quoted in this Catalogue (subject to being unsold) until 30 April 1991. After this date we will still supply the items where possible but there may be some price adjustments.

We regret, however, that commemorative stamps can only be supplied in complete sets and that orders totalling less than £5 (excluding postage) are respectfully declined.

To: Stanley Gibbons Ltd Great Britain Mail Order Service, 399 Strand, London WC2R 0LX

Please send me

SG No.	Condition (u/m, f/u, etc)	£	p	SG No.	Condition (u/m, f/u, etc)	£	p	SG No	Condition (u/m, f/u, etc.)	£	p

☐ I enclose cheque/PO made payable to Stanley Gibbons Ltd. for £...............

☐ I have paid £.......... into Stanley Gibbons Giro Account No. 586 6006

Total

Postage & Handling (£2.50 UK, £5 O/S)

Total Order Value

☐ I authorise you to charge my credit card for £...............

Type of card .... (all major cards accepted)   Expiry date

Card No.

Signature ....

Name ....Address ....

.... Postcode ....

Please allow 14 days for delivery (overseas customers 21 days)

REGIONAL ISSUES

PERFORATION AND WATERMARK. All the following Regional stamps are perforated 15×14 and are watermarked Type **179**, unless otherwise stated.

For listing of First Day Covers see pages 101/2.

1 Northern Ireland

N 1   N 2   N 3   N 4

1958–67

NI1	N **1**	3d lilac	20	10	☐	☐
		p. One centre phosphor band	20	15	☐	☐
NI2		4d blue	20	15	☐	☐
		p. Two phosphor bands ..	20	15	☐	☐
NI3	N **2**	6d purple	20	20	☐	☐
NI4		9d bronze-green (2 phosphor bands)	30	50	☐	☐
NI5	N **3**	1s 3d green	30	50	☐	☐
NI6		1s 6d blue (2 phosphor bands)	30	50	☐	☐

1968–69 One centre phosphor band (Nos. NI8/9) or two phosphor bands (others). No wmk

NI7	N **1**	4d blue	20	15	☐	☐
NI8		4d sepia	20	15	☐	☐
NI9		4d vermilion ..	20	20	☐	☐
NI10		5d blue	20	20	☐	☐
NI11	N **3**	1s 6d blue	2·50	3·00	☐	☐
		Presentation Pack (comprises Nos. NI1p, NI4/6, NI8/10) ..	3·00		☐	

Decimal Currency

1971–89 *Type N* **4** *No wmk*

(a) Printed in photogravure with phosphor bands

NI12	2½p magenta (1 centre band) ..	90	25	☐	☐
NI13	3p ultramarine (2 bands) ..	40	15	☐	☐
NI14	3p ultramarine (1 centre band) ..	20	15	☐	☐
NI15	3½p olive-grey (2 bands) ..	20	20	☐	☐
NI16	3½p olive-grey (1 centre band) ..	20	25	☐	☐
NI17	4½p grey-blue (2 bands) ..	25	25	☐	☐
NI18	5p violet (2 bands) ..	1·50	1·50	☐	☐
NI19	5½p violet (2 bands) ..	20	20	☐	☐
NI20	5½p violet (1 centre band) ..	20	20	☐	☐
NI21	6½p blue (1 centre band) ..	20	20	☐	☐

NI22	7p brown (1 centre band) ..	25	25	☐	☐
NI23	7½p chestnut (2 bands) ..	2·50	2·50	☐	☐
NI24	8p rosine (2 bands) ..	30	30	☐	☐
NI25	8½p yellow-green (2 bands)	30	30	☐	☐
NI26	9p violet (2 bands) ..	30	30	☐	☐
NI27	10p orange-brown (2 bands)	35	35	☐	☐
NI28	10p orange-brown (1 centre band)	35	35	☐	☐
NI29	10½p blue (2 bands) ..	40	40	☐	☐
NI30	11p scarlet (2 bands)	40	40	☐	☐

(b) Printed in photogravure on phosphorised paper

NI31	12p yellowish green	40	45	☐	☐
NI32	13½p purple-brown	60	70	☐	☐
NI33	15p ultramarine	45	50	☐	☐

(c) Printed in lithography. Perf 14 (11½p, 12½p, 14p, (No. NI38), 15½p, 16p, 18p, (No. NI44), 19½p, 20½p, 22p, (No. NI50), 26p, 28p) or 15 × 14 (others).

NI34	11½p drab (1 side band) ..	1·00	60	☐	☐
NI35	12p brt emer (1 side band) ..	50	50	☐	☐
NI36	12½p light emer (1 side band) ..	50	40	☐	☐
	a. Perf 15 × 14 ..	4·00	4·00	☐	☐
NI37	13p pale chest (1 side band) ..	50	35	☐	☐
NI38	14p grey-blue (phosphorised paper) ..	60	50	☐	☐
NI39	14p dp blue (1 centre band) ..	25	30	☐	☐
NI40	15p brt blue (1 centre band) ..	25	30	☐	☐
NI41	15½p pale violet (phosphorised paper) ..	60	65	☐	☐
NI42	16p drab (phosphorised paper) ..	1·00	1·00	☐	☐
	a. Perf 15 × 14 ..	3·50	1·00	☐	☐
NI43	17p grey-blue (phosphorised paper) ..	60	40	☐	☐
NI44	18p dp violet (phosphorised paper) ..	80	80	☐	☐
NI45	18p olive-grey (phosphorised paper) ..	60	45	☐	☐
NI46	19p bright orange-red (phosphorised paper)	30	35	☐	☐
NI47	19½p olive-grey (phosphorised paper) ..	2·00	2·00	☐	☐
NI48	20p brownish black (phosphorised paper) ..	30	30	☐	☐
NI49	20½p ultramarine (phosphorised paper) ..	1·60	1·50	☐	☐
NI50	22p blue (phosphorised paper)	90	1·10	☐	☐
NI51	22p yellow-green (phosphorised paper) ..	35	50	☐	☐
NI52	23p bright green (phosphorised paper) ..	35	40	☐	☐
NI53	24p Indian red (phosphorised paper)	40	45	☐	☐
NI54	26p rosine (phosphorised paper) ..	80	80	☐	☐
	a. Perf 15 × 14	70	60	☐	☐
NI55	28p deep violet-blue (phosphorised paper) ..	85	80	☐	☐
	a. Perf 15 × 14	45	65	☐	☐
NI56	31p bright purple (phosphorised paper)	1·00	80	☐	☐

NI57	32p	greenish blue (phosphorised paper)	50	60 □ □	
NI58	34p	dp bluish grey (phosphorised paper)	55	55 □ □	

Presentation Pack (*contains* 2½p (NI12), 3p (NI13), 5p (NI18), 7½p (NI23)) .. .. 4·00 □

Presentation Pack (*contains* 3p (NI14), 3½p (NI15), 5½p (NI19), 8p (NI24) *later with* 4½p (NI17) *added*) .. .. 3·00 □

Presentation Pack (*contains* 6½p (NI21), 8½p (NI25), 10p (NI27), 11p (NI30)) .. .. 1·75 □

Presentation Pack (*contains* 7p (NI22), 9p (NI26), 10½p (NI29), 11½p (NI34), 12p (NI31), 13½p (NI32), 14p (NI38), 15p (NI33), 18p (NI44), 22p (NI50)) .. 6·00 □

Presentation Pack (*contains* 10p (NI28), 12½p (NI36), 16p (NI42), 20½p (NI49), 26p (NI54), 28p (NI55)) .. 5·00 □

Presentation Pack (*contains* 10p (NI28), 13p (NI37), 16p (NI42a), 17p (NI43), 22p (NI51), 26p (NI54), 28p (NI55), 31p (NI56)) .. 8·00 □

Presentation Pack (*contains* 12p (NI35), 13p (NI37), 17p (NI43), 20½p (NI45), 22p (NI51), 26p (NI54a), 28p (NI55a), 31p (NI56)) .. 3·00 □

Presentation Pack (*contains* 14p, 19p, 23p, 32p *from Northern Ireland, Scotland and Wales* (*Nos.* NI39, NI46, NI52, NI57, S54, S59, S63, S69, W40, W47, W53, W58)) 4·25 □

Presentation Pack (*contains* 15p, 20p, 24p, 34p *from Northern Ireland, Scotland and Wales* (*Nos.* NI40, NI48, NI53, NI58, S56, S61, S65, S70, W41, W49, W54, W59) .. .. 5·00 □

2 Scotland

| S 1 | S 2 | S 3 | S 4 |

1958–67

S1	S 1	3d	lilac	20	15 □ □	
		p.	*Two phosphor bands* ..	17·00	1·00 □ □	
		pa.	*One side band*	20	25 □ □	
		pb.	*One centre band*	20	15 □ □	
S2		4d	blue	20	10 □ □	
		p.	*Two phosphor bands* ..	20	20 □ □	
S3	S 2	6d	purple	20	15 □ □	
		p.	*Two phosphor bands* ..	20	25 □ □	
S4		9d	bronze-green (2 phosphor bands)	30	30 □ □	
S5	S 3	1s 3d	green	30	30 □ □	
		p.	*Two phosphor bands* ..	30	30 □ □	
S6		1s 6d	blue (2 phosphor bands)	35	30 □ □	

No. S1*pa* exists with the phosphor band at the left or right of the stamp.

1967–70 *One centre phosphor band* (*Nos.* S7, S9/10) *or two phosphor bands* (*others*). *No wmk*

S7	S 1	3d	lilac	10	15 □ □	
S8		4d	blue	10	15 □ □	
S9		4d	sepia	10	10 □ □	
S10		4d	vermilion ..	10	10 □ □	
S11		5d	blue	20	10 □ □	
S12	S 2	9d	bronze-green ..	5·00	5·50 □ □	
S13	S 3	1s 6d	blue	1·40	1·00 □ □	
			Presentation Pack (*containing Nos.* S3, S5p, S7, S9/13) ..	13·00	□	

Decimal Currency

1971–89 *Type* S 4. *No wmk*

(a) *Printed in photogravure by Harrison and Sons with phosphor bands. Perf* 15 × 14.

S14	2½p	magenta (1 centre band)	20	15 □ □
S15	3p	ultramarine (2 bands) ..	30	15 □ □
S16	3p	ultramarine (1 centre band)	15	15 □ □
S17	3½p	olive-grey (2 bands) ..	20	20 □ □
S18	3½p	ol-grey (1 centre band)	20	20 □ □
S19	4½p	grey-blue (2 bands) ..	25	20 □ □
S20	5p	violet (2 bands)	1·50	1·50 □ □
S21	5½p	violet (2 bands)	20	20 □ □
S22	5½p	violet (1 centre band) ..	20	20 □ □
S23	6½p	blue (1 centre band) ..	20	20 □ □

S24	7p brown (1 centre band)	25	25	☐	☐	
S25	7½p chestnut (2 bands) ..	2·00	2·00	☐	☐	
S26	8p rosine (2 bands) ..	30	40	☐	☐	
S27	8½p yellow-green (2 bands)	30	30	☐	☐	
S28	9p violet (2 bands)	30	30	☐	☐	
S29	10p orange-brown (2 bands)	35	30	☐	☐	
S30	10p orange-brown (1 centre band)	35	35	☐	☐	
S31	10½p blue (2 bands) ..	40	35	☐	☐	
S32	11p scarlet (2 bands) ..	40	35	☐	☐	

(b) Printed in photogravure by Harrison and Sons on phosphorised paper. Perf 15 × 14

S33	12p yellowish green	40	30	☐	☐	
S34	13½p purple-brown	60	65	☐	☐	
S35	15p ultramarine	45	45	☐	☐	

(c) Printed in lithography by John Waddington. One side phosphor band (11½p, 12p, 12½p, 13p) or phosphorised paper (others). Perf 13½ × 14

S36	11½p drab	75	60	☐	☐	
S37	12p bright emerald	55	70	☐	☐	
S38	12½p light emerald	40	40	☐	☐	
S39	13p pale chestnut	40	30	☐	☐	
S40	14p grey-blue	55	50	☐	☐	
S41	15½p pale violet	60	65	☐	☐	
S42	16p drab	55	45	☐	☐	
S43	17p grey-blue	70	1·00	☐	☐	
S44	18p deep violet	70	65	☐	☐	
S45	19½p olive-grey	2·00	2·25	☐	☐	
S46	20½p ultramarine	1·60	1·50	☐	☐	
S47	22p blue	80	1·10	☐	☐	
S48	22p yellow-green	80	80	☐	☐	
S49	26p rosine	80	80	☐	☐	
S50	28p deep violet-blue ..	85	80	☐	☐	
S51	31p bright purple ..	80	90	☐	☐	

(d) Printed in lithography by Questa. Perf 15 × 14

S52	12p brt emer (1 side band) ..	50	60	☐	☐	
S53	13p pale chest (1 side band) ..	50	30	☐	☐	
S54	14p dp bl (1 centre band)	25	30	☐	☐	
S55	14p deep blue (1 side band) ..	50	50	☐	☐	
S56	15p bright blue (1 centre band)	25	30	☐	☐	
S57	17p grey-bl (phosphorised paper) ..	3·00	2·00	☐	☐	
S58	18p ol-grey (phosphorised paper)	60	45	☐	☐	
S59	19p bright orange-red (phosphorised paper) ..	30	35	☐	☐	
S60	19p brt orge-red (2 bands) ..	1·00	1·00	☐	☐	
S61	20p brownish black (phosphorised paper) ..	30	30	☐	☐	
S62	22p yell-grn (phosphorised paper)	35	50	☐	☐	
S63	23p brt grn (phosphorised paper)	35	40	☐	☐	
S64	23p bright green (2 bands) ..	3·00	3·00	☐	☐	
S65	24p Indian red (phosphorised paper)	40	45	☐	☐	
S66	26p rosine (phosphorised paper)	80	80	☐	☐	

S67	28p deep violet-blue (phosphorised paper) ..	45	65	☐	☐	
S68	31p bright purple (phosphorised paper) ..	65	70	☐	☐	
S69	32p greenish blue (phosphorised paper) ..	50	60	☐	☐	
S70	34p dp bluish grey (phosphorised paper)	55	55	☐	☐	
	Presentation Pack (contains 2½p (S14), 3p (S15), 5p (S20), 7½p (S25))	4·00		☐		
	Presentation Pack (contains 3p (S16), 3½p (S17), 5½p (S21), 8p (S26) later with 4½p (S19) added)	3·00		☐		
	Presentation Pack (contains 6½p (S23), 8½p (S27), 10p (S29), 11p (S32))	1·75		☐		
	Presentation Pack (contains 7p (S24), 9p (S28), 10½p (S31), 11½p (S36), 12p (S33), 13½p (S34), 14p (S40), 15p (S35), 18p (S44), 22p (S47))	6·00		☐		
	Presentation Pack (contains 10p (S30), 12½p (S38), 16p (S42), 20½p (S46), 26p (S49), 28p (S50))	5·00		☐		
	Presentation Pack (contains 10p (S30), 13p (S39), 16p (S42), 17p (S43), 22p (S48), 26p (S49), 28p (S50), 31p (S51))	8·00		☐		
	Presentation Pack (contains 12p (S52), 13p (S53), 17p (S57), 18p (S58), 22p (S62), 26p (S66), 28p (S67), 31p (S68))	3·00		☐		

For combined packs containing values from all three Regions see under Northern Ireland.

3 Wales and Monmouthshire

W 1   W 2   W 3   W 4

1958–67

W1	W 1	3d lilac	20	10	☐	☐
		p. One centre phosphor band ..	15	15	☐	☐
W2		4d blue	15	12	☐	☐
		p. Two phosphor bands	15	12	☐	☐
W3	W 2	6d purple	20	20	☐	☐
W4		9d bronze-green (2 phosphor bands)	30	35	☐	☐
W5	W 3	1s 3d green	30	30	☐	☐
W6		1s 6d blue (2 phosphor bands)	35	30	☐	☐

1967–69 *One centre phosphor band (Nos. W7, W9/10) or two phosphor bands (others). No wmk*

W7	W 1	3d lilac	20	10	☐	☐
W8		4d blue	20	10	☐	☐
W9		4d sepia	20	10	☐	☐
W10		4d vermilion ..	20	20	☐	☐
W11		5d blue	20	10	☐	☐
W12	W 3	1s 6d blue	3·00	3·00	☐	☐
		Presentation Pack (comprises Nos. W4, W6/7, W9/11) ..	2·50		☐	

Decimal Currency

1971–89 *Type W 4. No wmk*

(a) Printed in photogravure with phosphor bands

W13	2½p magenta (1 centre band)	20	15	☐	☐
W14	3p ultramarine (2 bands) ..	25	15	☐	☐
W15	3p ultramarine (1 centre band) ..	20	20	☐	☐
W16	3½p olive-grey (2 bands) ..	20	25	☐	☐
W17	3½p olive-grey (1 centre band) ..	20	25	☐	☐
W18	4½p grey-blue (2 bands) ..	25	20	☐	☐
W19	5p violet (2 bands) ..	1·50	1·50	☐	☐
W20	5½p violet (2 bands) ..	20	25	☐	☐
W21	5½p violet (1 centre band) ..	20	25	☐	☐
W22	6½p blue (1 centre band) ..	20	20	☐	☐
W23	7p brown (1 centre band) ..	25	25	☐	☐
W24	7½p chestnut (2 bands) ..	2·00	2·25	☐	☐
W25	8p rosine (2 bands) ..	30	30	☐	☐
W26	8½p yellow-green (2 bands) ..	30	30	☐	☐
W27	9p violet (2 bands) ..	30	30	☐	☐

W28	10p orange-brown (2 bands)	35	30	☐	☐
W29	10p orange-brown (1 centre band)	35	30	☐	☐
W30	10½p blue (2 bands)	40	35	☐	☐
W31	11p scarlet (2 bands)	40	45	☐	☐

(b) Printed in photogravure on phosphorised paper

W32	12p yellowish green	40	45	☐	☐
W33	13½p purple-brown	60	70	☐	☐
W34	15p ultramarine	45	50	☐	☐

(c) Printed in lithography. Perf 14 (11½p, 12½p, 14p (No. W39), 15½p, 16p, 18p (No. W45), 19½p, 20½p, 22p (No. W51), 26p, 28p) or 15 × 14 (others).

W35	11½p drab (1 side band)	75	60	☐	☐
W36	12p brt emer (1 side band) ..	1·00	1·00	☐	☐
W37	12½p light emer (1 side band)..	50	45	☐	☐
	a. Perf 15 × 14	4·50	3·75	☐	☐
W38	13p pale chest (1 side band)..	40	35	☐	☐
W39	14p grey-blue (phosphorised paper)	55	50	☐	☐
W40	14p dp blue (1 centre band) ..	25	30	☐	☐
W41	15p brt blue (1 centre band) ..	25	30	☐	☐
W42	15½p pale violet (phosphorised paper)	60	65	☐	☐
W43	16p drab (phosphorised paper)	1·00	1·00	☐	☐
	a. Perf 15 × 14	80	1·00	☐	☐
W44	17p grey-blue (phosphorised paper)	60	45	☐	☐
W45	18p deep violet (phosphorised paper)	70	75	☐	☐
W46	18p olive-grey (phosphor-ised paper)	60	45	☐	☐
W47	19p bright orange-red (phos-phorised paper)	30	35	☐	☐
W48	19½p olive-grey (phosphorised paper)	2·00	2·00	☐	☐
W49	20p brownish black (phos-phorised paper)	30	30	☐	☐
W50	20½p ultramarine (phosphor-ised paper)	1·60	1·50	☐	☐
W51	22p blue (phosphorised paper)	80	1·10	☐	☐
W52	22p yell-green (phosphorised paper)	35	50	☐	☐
W53	23p brt green (phosphorised paper)	35	40	☐	☐
W54	24p Indian red (phosphorised paper)	40	45	☐	☐
W55	26p rosine (phosphorised paper)	80	80	☐	☐
	a. Perf 15 × 14	1·00	60	☐	☐
W56	28p dp viol-blue (phosphor-ised paper)	85	80	☐	☐
	a. Perf 15 × 14	45	65	☐	☐
W57	31p brt purple (phosphorised paper)	90	70	☐	☐
W58	32p greenish blue (phosphor-ised paper)	55	60	☐	☐
W59	34p deep bluish grey (phosphorised paper) ..	55	55	☐	☐

Presentation Pack (*contains*
2½p (W13), 3p (W14), 5p
(W19), 7½p (W24)) .. .. 4·00 □

Presentation Pack (*contains* 3p
(W15), 3½p (W16), 5½p
(W20), 8p (W25), *later with*
4½p (W18) *added*) .. .. 3·00 □

Presentation Pack (*contains*
6½p (W22), 8½p (W26), 10p
(W28), 11p (W31)) .. .. 1·75 □

Presentation Pack (*contains* 7p
(W23), 9p (W27), 10½p
(W30), 11½p (W35), 12p
(W32), 13½p (W33), 14p
(W39), 15p (W34), 18p
(W45), 22p (W51)) .. .. 6·00 □

Presentation Pack (*contains*
10p (W29), 12½p (W37), 16p
(W43), 20½p (W50), 26p
(W55), 28p (W56)) .. .. 5·00 □

Presentation Pack (*contains*
10p (W29), 13p (W38), 16p
(W43*a*), 17p (W44), 22p
(W52), 26p (W55), 28p·
(W56), 31p (W57)) .. .. 8·50 □

Presentation Pack (*contains*
12p (W36), 13p (W38), 17p
(W44), 18p (W46), 22p
(W52), 26p (W55*a*), 28p
(W56*a*), 31p (W57)) .. .. 3·00 □

For combined packs containing values from all three Regions
see under Northern Ireland.

ISLE OF MAN
Regional Issues

1   2   3

1958–67 *Wmk* **179**   *Perf* 15 × 14

1	1	2½d red	.. ..	45	80	□ □
2	2	3d lilac	.. ..	20	10	□ □
		p. One centre phosphor band		20	30	□ □
3		4d blue	.. ..	1·50	1·10	□ □
		p. Two phosphor bands	..	20	15	□ □

1968–69 *One centre phosphor band (Nos.* 5/6) *or two
phosphor bands (others). No wmk*

4	2	4d blue	..	20	25	□ □
5		4d sepia	..	20	30	□ □
6		4d vermilion	..	45	60	□ □
7		5d blue	..	45	60	□ □

Decimal Currency

1971 (7 JULY) *One centre phosphor band* (2½p) *or two
phosphor bands (others). No wmk*

8	3	2½p magenta	.. ..	20	15	□ □
9		3p ultramarine	..	20	15	□ □
10		5p violet	.. ..	70	75	□ □
11		7½p chestnut	.. ..	70	90	□ □
		Presentation Pack	.. ..	2·00		□

For comprehensive listings of the Independent Administration
issues of the Isle of Man, see Stanley Gibbons *Collect Channel
Islands and Isle of Man Stamps.*

CHANNEL ISLANDS
1 General Issue

C 1 Gathering Vraic   C 2 Islanders gathering Vraic

Third Anniversary of Liberation

1948 (10 MAY) *Wmk Type* **127**   *Perf* 15 × 14

CI	C 1	1d red	.. .. ..	20	20	□ □
C2	C 2	2½d blue	.. ..	30	30	□ □
		First Day Cover	.. .. ..		15·00	□

2 Guernsey

(a) War Occupation Issues

Stamps issued under British authority during the German Occupation.

1   2   3

1941–44 *Rouletted.* (a) *White paper. No wmk*

1	1	½d green	..	..	3·00	2·50	□ □
2		1d red ..	..	..	2·25	1·25	□ □
3a		2½d blue	..	..	6·00	6·00	□ □

(b) *Bluish French bank-note paper. Wmk loops*

4	1	½d green	..	..	14·00	22·00	□ □
5		1d red ..	..	..	8·00	22·00	□ □

(b) Regional Issues

1958–67 *Wmk* 179   *Perf* 15 × 14

6	2	2½d red ..	..	..	35	40	□ □
7	3	3d lilac	..	..	35	30	□ □
		p. One centre phosphor band			20	20	□ □
8		4d blue	..	..	25	30	□ □
		p. Two phosphor bands	..	..	20	20	□ □

1968–69 *One centre phosphor band (Nos. 10/11) or two phosphor bands (others). No wmk*

9	3	4d blue	..	..	10	25	□ □
10		4d sepia	..	..	15	20	□ □
11		4d vermilion	..	..	15	30	□ □
12		5d blue	..	..	15	30	□ □

For comprehensive listings of the Independent Postal Administration issues of Guernsey, see Stanley Gibbons *Collect Channel Islands and Isle of Man Stamps.*

3 Jersey

(a) War Occupation Issues

Stamps issued under British authority during the German Occupation.

1   2 Old Jersey Farm   3 Portelet Bay

4 Corbière Lighthouse   5 Elizabeth Castle

6 Mont Orgueil Castle   7 Gathering Vraic
                                    (seaweed)

1941–42 *White paper. No wmk   Perf* 11

1	1	½d green	..	..	3·75	2·50	□ □
2		1d red ..	..	..	4·00	3·50	□ □

1943 *No wmk   Perf* 13½

3	2	½d green	..	..	7·00	3·75	□ □
4	3	1d red ..	..	..	1·00	50	□ □
5	4	1½d brown	..	..	3·00	3·00	□ □
6	5	2d orange	..	..	3·00	2·25	□ □
7a	6	2½d blue	..	..	1·00	2·00	□ □
8	7	3d violet	..	..	1·00	4·00	□ □
		Set of 6	..	..	14·00	14·00	□ □

(b) Regional Issues

8   9

1958–67 *Wmk* 179   *Perf* 15 × 14

9	8	2½d red ..	..	..	35	50	□ □
10	9	3d lilac	..	..	35	30	□ □
		p. One centre phospnor band			20	20	□ □
11		4d blue	..	..	25	30	□ □
		p. Two phosphor bands	..	..	20	25	□ □

1968–69 *One centre phosphor band (4d values) or two phosphor bands (5d). No wmk*

12	9	4d sepia	..	..	20	25	□ □
13		4d vermilion	..	..	20	30	□ □
14		5d blue	..	..	20	40	□ □

For comprehensive listings of the Independent Postal Administration issues of Jersey, see Stanley Gibbons *Collect Channel Islands and Isle of Man Stamps.*

REGIONAL FIRST DAY COVERS

PRICES for First Day Covers listed below are for stamps, as indicated, used on illustrated envelopes and postmarked with operational cancellations (before 1964) or with special First Day of Issue cancellations (1964 onwards). First Day postmarks of 8 June 1964 and 7 February 1966 were of the machine cancellation "envelope" type.

£sd Issues

18 Aug. 1958	*Guernsey 3d (No. 7)*	7·50 ☐
	Isle of Man 3d (No. 2)	13·00 ☐
	Jersey 3d (No. 10)..	10·00 ☐
	Northern Ireland 3d (No. NI1)	11·00 ☐
	Scotland 3d (No. S1)	5·00 ☐
	Wales 3d (No. W1)	5·00 ☐
29 Sept. 1958	*Northern Ireland 6d, 1s 3d (Nos. NI3, NI5)*	14·00 ☐
	Scotland 6d, 1s 3d (Nos S3, S5)	12·00 ☐
	Wales 6d, 1s 3d (Nos. W3, W5)	10·00 ☐
8 June 1964	*Guernsey 2½d (No. 6)*	12·00 ☐
	Isle of Man 2½d (No. 1)	13·00 ☐
	Jersey 2½d (No. 9) ..	12·00 ☐
7 Feb. 1966	*Guernsey 4d (No. 8)*	5·00 ☐
	Isle of Man 4d (No. 3)	5·00 ☐
	Jersey 4d (No. 11)..	5·00 ☐
	Northern Ireland 4d (No. NI2)	3·00 ☐
	Scotland 4d (No. S2)	3·00 ☐
	Wales 4d (No. W2)	3·00 ☐
1 March 1967	*Northern Ireland 9d, 1s 6d (Nos. NI4, NI6)*	1·50 ☐
	Scotland 9d, 1s 6d (Nos. S4, S6)	1·50 ☐
	Wales 9d, 1s 6d (Nos. W4, W6)	1·50 ☐
4 Sept. 1968	*Guernsey 4d, 5d (Nos. 10, 12)*	1·00 ☐
	Isle of Man 4d, 5d (Nos. 5, 7)	1·75 ☐
	Jersey 4d, 5d (Nos. 12, 14)	1·25 ☐
	Northern Ireland 4d, 5d (Nos. NI8, NI10)	50 ☐
	Scotland 4d, 5d (Nos. S9, S11)	50 ☐
	Wales 4d, 5d (Nos. W9, W11)	50 ☐

Decimal Issues

7 July 1971	*Isle of Man 2½p, 3p, 5p, 7½p (Nos. 8/11)*	3·50 ☐
	Northern Ireland 2½p, 3p, 5p, 7½p (Nos. NI12/13, NI18, NI23)	4·00 ☐
	Scotland 2½p, 3p, 5p, 7½p (Nos. S14/15, S20, S25)	4·00 ☐
	Wales 2½p, 3p, 5p, 7½p (Nos. W13/14, W19, W24)	4·00 ☐
23 Jan. 1974	*Northern Ireland 3p, 3½p, 5½p, 8p (Nos. NI14/15, NI19, NI24)*	1·50 ☐
	Scotland 3p, 3½p, 5½p, 8p (Nos. S16/17, S21, S26)	1·50 ☐
	Wales 3p, 3½p, 5½p, 8p (Nos. W15/16, W20, W25)	1·50 ☐

6 Nov. 1974	*Northern Ireland 4½p, (No. NI17)*	1·00 ☐
	Scotland 4½p (No. S19)	1·00 ☐
	Wales 4½p (No. W18)	1·00 ☐
14 Jan. 1976	*Northern Ireland 6½p, 8½p (Nos. NI21, NI25)*	60 ☐
	Scotland 6½p, 8½p (Nos. S23, S27)	60 ☐
	Wales 6½p, 8½p (Nos. W22, W26)	60 ☐
20 Oct. 1976	*Northern Ireland 10p, 11p (Nos. NI27, NI30)*	1·00 ☐
	Scotland 10p, 11p (Nos. S29, S32)	1·00 ☐
	Wales 10p, 11p (Nos. W28, W31)	1·00 ☐
18 Jan. 1978	*Northern Ireland 7p, 9p, 10½p (Nos. NI22, NI26, NI29)* ..	1·00 ☐
	Scotland 7p, 9p, 10½p (Nos. S24, S28, S31)	1·00 ☐
	Wales 7p, 9p, 10½p (Nos. W23, W27, W30)	1·00 ☐
23 July 1980	*Northern Ireland 12p, 13½p, 15p (Nos. NI31/3)*	2·00 ☐
	Scotland 12p, 13½p, 15p (Nos. S33/5)	2·00 ☐
	Wales 12p, 13½p, 15p (Nos. W32/4)	2·00 ☐
8 April 1981	*Northern Ireland 11½p, 14p, 18p, 22p (Nos. NI34, NI38, NI44, NI50)*	2·00 ☐
	Scotland 11½p, 14p, 18p, 22p (Nos. S36, S40, S44, S47)	2·00 ☐
	Wales 11½p, 14p, 18p, 22p (Nos. W35, W39, W45, W51)	2·00 ☐
24 Feb. 1982	*Northern Ireland 12½p, 15½p, 19½p, 26p (Nos. NI36, NI41, NI47, NI54)*	3·00 ☐
	Scotland 12½p, 15½p, 19½p, 26p (Nos. S38, S41, S45, S49)	3·00 ☐
	Wales 12½p, 15½p, 19½p, 26p (Nos. W37, W42, W48, W55) ..	3·00 ☐
27 April 1983	*Northern Ireland 16p, 20½p, 28p (Nos. NI42, NI49, NI55)*	3·00 ☐
	Scotland 16p, 20½p, 28p (Nos. S42, S46, S50)	3·00 ☐
	Wales 16p, 20½p, 28p (Nos. W43, W50, W56) ..	3·00 ☐
23 Oct. 1984	*Northern Ireland 13p, 17p, 22p, 31p (Nos. NI37, NI43, NI51, NI56)*	4·50 ☐
	Scotland 13p, 17p, 22p, 31p (Nos. S39, S43, S48, S51) ..	5·00 ☐
	Wales 13p, 17p, 22p, 31p (Nos. W38, W44, W52, W57)	4·50 ☐

Date	Description				Price	
7 Jan. 1986	*Northern Ireland* 12p					
	(*No.* NI35)	1·25	☐			
	Scotland 12p (*No.* S37)	1·25	☐			
	Wales 12p (*No.* W36) ..	1·25	☐			
6 Jan. 1987	*Northern Ireland* 18p					
	(*No.* NI45)	1·75	☐			
	Scotland 18p (*No.* S58)	1·75	☐			
	Wales 18p (*No.* W46)	1·75	☐			
8 Nov. 1988	*Northern Ireland* 14p, 19p, 23p, 32p (*Nos.* NI39, NI46, NI52, NI57)	3·00	☐			
	Scotland 14p, 19p, 23p, 32p (*Nos.* S54, S59, S64, S69) ..	3·00	☐			
	Wales 14p, 19p, 23p, 32p (*Nos.* W40, W47, W53, W58) ..	3·00	☐			
28 Nov. 1989	*Northern Ireland* 15p, 20p, 24p, 34p (*Nos.* NI40, NI48, NI53, NI58)	2·25	☐			
	Scotland 15p, 20p, 24p, 34p (*Nos.* S56, S61, S65, S70) ..	2·25	☐			
	Wales 15p, 20p, 24p, 34p (*Nos.* W41, W49, W54, W59)	2·25	☐			

POSTAGE DUE STAMPS

PERFORATION. All postage due stamps are perf 14 × 15.

D 1

D 2

1914–23 *Wmk Type* **96** (*Royal Cypher* (*'Simple'*)) *sideways*

No.	Type	Value	Colour			Un	Used		
D1	D 1	½d	green	..	..	40	40	☐	☐
D2		1d	red	..	..	50	40	☐	☐
D3		1½d	brown	..	..	40·00	15·00	☐	☐
D4		2d	black	..	..	50	40	☐	☐
D5		3d	violet	..	..	2·00	1·00	☐	☐
D6		4d	green	..	..	25·00	1·75	☐	☐
D7		5d	brown	..	..	2·50	1·50	☐	☐
D8		1s	blue	..	..	25·00	2·00	☐	☐
		Set of 8	..	..	..	85·00	20·00	☐	☐

1924–31 *Wmk Type* **107** (*Block* G v R) *sideways*

No.	Type	Value	Colour			Un	Used		
D10	D 1	½d	green	..	..	30	30	☐	☐
D11		1d	red ..		..	50	30	☐	☐
D12		1½d	brown	..	..	35·00	15·00	☐	☐
D13		2d	black	..	..	1·60	40	☐	☐
D14		3d	violet	..	..	2·00	40	☐	☐
D15		4d	green	..	..	12·00	2·00	☐	☐
D16		5d	brown	..	..	21·00	25·00	☐	☐
D17		1s	blue	..	..	8·00	75	☐	☐
D18	D 2	2s 6d	purple/*yellow*	..		60·00	1·75	☐	☐
		Set of 9	..	.. ..	..	£125	42·00	☐	☐

1936–37 *Wmk Type* **125** (E 8 R) *sideways*

No.	Type	Value	Colour			Un	Used		
D19	D 1	½d	green	..	..	5·50	5·00	☐	☐
D20		1d	red ..		..	1·00	1·60	☐	☐
D21		2d	black	..	..	7·50	5·00	☐	☐
D22		3d	violet	..	..	1·60	1·60	☐	☐
D23		4d	green	..	..	12·00	15·00	☐	☐
D24a		5d	brown	..	..	12·00	15·00	☐	☐
D25		1s	blue	..	..	7·50	4·50	☐	☐
D26	D 2	2s 6d	purple/*yellow*	..		£160	8·00	☐	☐
		Set of 8	..	.. ..	..	£180	55·00	☐	☐

1937–38 *Wmk Type* **127** (G VI R) *sideways*

No.	Type	Value	Colour			Un	Used		
D27	D 1	½d	green	..	..	7·00	3·25	☐	☐
D28		1d	red ..		..	1·75	40	☐	☐
D29		2d	black	..	..	1·75	40	☐	☐
D30		3d	violet	..	..	8·00	40	☐	☐
D31		4d	green	..	..	45·00	7·50	☐	☐
D32		5d	brown	..	..	7·00	1·50	☐	☐
D33		1s	blue	..	..	48·00	1·00	☐	☐
D34	D 2	2s 6d	purple/*yellow*	..		55·00	3·00	☐	☐
		Set of 8	..	.. ..	..	£150	15·00	☐	☐

1951–52 *Colours changed and new value* (1½d). *Wmk Type* **127** (G VI R) *sideways*

No.	Type	Value	Colour			Un	Used		
D35	D 1	½d	orange	..	..	1·75	2·00	☐	☐
D36		1d	blue	..	..	1·10	75	☐	☐
D37		1½d	green	..	..	1·75	1·75	☐	☐
D38		4d	blue	..	..	28·00	9·00	☐	☐
D39		1s	brown	..	..	28·00	4·00	☐	☐
		Set of 5	..	.. ..	..	55·00	16·00	☐	☐

1954–55 *Wmk Type* **153** (*Mult. Tudor Crown and* E 2 R) *sideways*

D40	D 1	½d orange	3·00	2·50 ☐ ☐	
D41		2d black	1·90	2·00 ☐ ☐	
D42		3d violet	40·00	25·00 ☐ ☐	
D43		4d blue	15·00	16·00 ☐ ☐	
D44		5d brown	17·00	6·50 ☐ ☐	
D45	D 2	2s 6d purple/*yellow* ..	£120	3·00 ☐ ☐	
		Set of 6	£175	50·00 ☐ ☐	

1955–57 *Wmk Type* **165** (*Mult. St Edward's Crown and* E 2 R) *sideways*

D46	D 1	½d orange	1·50	2·25 ☐ ☐	
D47		1d blue	4·00	1·25 ☐ ☐	
D48		1½d green	3·75	3·75 ☐ ☐	
D49		2d black	35·00	3·00 ☐ ☐	
D50		3d violet	4·50	1·25 ☐ ☐	
D51		4d blue	18·00	3·00 ☐ ☐	
D52		5d brown	27·00	2·00 ☐ ☐	
D53		1s brown	65·00	1·25 ☐ ☐	
D54	D 2	2s 6d purple/*yellow* ..	£160	7·50 ☐ ☐	
D55		5s red/*yellow* ..	90·00	19·00 ☐ ☐	
		Set of 10	£375	40·00 ☐ ☐	

1959–63 *Wmk Type* **179** (*Mult. St Edward's Crown*) *sideways*

D56	D 1	½d orange	10	45 ☐ ☐	
D57		1d blue	10	15 ☐ ☐	
D58		1½d green	90	1·50 ☐ ☐	
D59		2d black	1·25	30 ☐ ☐	
D60		3d violet	40	15 ☐ ☐	
D61		4d blue	40	20 ☐ ☐	
D62		5d brown	45	45 ☐ ☐	
D63		6d purple	60	30 ☐ ☐	
D64		1s brown	1·40	25 ☐ ☐	
D65	D 2	2s 6d purple/*yellow* ..	4·00	45 ☐ ☐	
D66		5s red/*yellow* ..	7·50	70 ☐ ☐	
D67		10s blue/*yellow* ..	9·00	3·75 ☐ ☐	
D68		£1 black/*yellow* ..	45·00	7·00 ☐ ☐	
		Set of 13	60·00	14·00 ☐ ☐	

1968–69 *Design size* 22½ × 19 *mm No wmk*

D69	D 1	2d black	40	40 ☐ ☐	
D70		3d violet	25	40 ☐ ☐	
D71		4d blue	25	40 ☐ ☐	
D72		5d orange-brown ..	4·50	5·25 ☐ ☐	
D73		6d purple	80	60 ☐ ☐	
D74		1s brown	80	1·00 ☐ ☐	
		Set of 6	6·50	7·00 ☐ ☐	

1968–69 *Design size* 21½ × 17½ *mm No wmk*

D75	D 1	4d blue	5·00	5·00 ☐ ☐	
D76		8d red	1·25	75 ☐ ☐	

D 3

D 4

Decimal Currency

1970–77 *No wmk*

D77	D 3	½p turquoise-blue	10	20 ☐ ☐	
D78		1p reddish purple	10	15 ☐ ☐	
D79		2p myrtle-green ..	10	15 ☐ ☐	
D80		3p ultramarine ..	15	10 ☐ ☐	
D81		4p yellow-brown ..	15	15 ☐ ☐	
D82		5p violet	20	20 ☐ ☐	
D83		7p red-brown ..	35	45 ☐ ☐	
D84	D 4	10p red	30	20 ☐ ☐	
D85		11p green	50	60 ☐ ☐	
D86		20p brown	60	50 ☐ ☐	
D87		50p ultramarine ..	1·50	40 ☐ ☐	
D88		£1 black	2·75	60 ☐ ☐	
D89		£5 orange-yellow and black	20·00	2·00 ☐ ☐	
		Set of 13	25·00	5·00 ☐ ☐	

D77/82, D84, D86/8 *Presentation Pack* .. .. 10·00 ☐

D77/88 *Presentation Pack* .. .. 6·00 ☐

D 5

D 6

1982 *No wmk*

D 90	D 5	1p lake	10	10 ☐ ☐	
D 91		2p bright blue ..	10	10 ☐ ☐	
D 92		3p deep mauve ..	10	15 ☐ ☐	
D 93		4p deep blue	10	20 ☐ ☐	
D 94		5p sepia	10	20 ☐ ☐	
D 95	D 6	10p light brown ..	15	25 ☐ ☐	
D 96		20p olive-green ..	30	30 ☐ ☐	
D 97		25p deep greenish blue ..	40	70 ☐ ☐	
D 98		50p grey-black ..	75	1·00 ☐ ☐	
D 99		£1 red	1·50	80 ☐ ☐	
D100		£2 turquoise-blue ..	3·00	2·00 ☐ ☐	
D101		£5 dull orange ..	7·50	1·50 ☐ ☐	
		Set of 12	12·50	6·50 ☐ ☐	
		Set of 12 *Gutter Pairs* ..	30·00	☐	
		Presentation Pack	14·00	☐	

ROYAL MAIL POSTAGE LABELS

These imperforate labels were issued as an experiment by the Post Office. Special microprocessor controlled machines were installed at post offices in Cambridge, London, Shirley (Southampton) and Windsor to provide an after-hours sales service to the public. The machines printed and dispensed the labels according to the coins inserted and the buttons operated by the customer. Values were initially available in $\frac{1}{2}$p steps to 16p and in addition, the labels were sold at philatelic counters in two packs containing either 3 values ($3\frac{1}{2}$, $12\frac{1}{2}$, 16p) or 32 values ($\frac{1}{2}$p to 16p).

From 28 August 1984 the machines were adjusted to provide values up to 17p. After 31 December 1984 labels including $\frac{1}{2}$p values were withdrawn. The machines were taken out of service on 30 April 1985.

Machine postage-paid impression in red on phosphorised paper with grey-green background design. No watermark. Imperforate.

1984 (1 May–28 Aug)

Set of 32 ($\frac{1}{2}$p to 16p)	..	28·00	30·00	☐ ☐
Set of 3 ($3\frac{1}{2}$p, $12\frac{1}{2}$p, 16p)	..	4·00	4·50	☐ ☐
Set of 3 on First Day Cover				
(1 May)			6·50	☐
Set of 2 ($16\frac{1}{2}$p, 17p)				
(28 August)		3·00	3·50	☐ ☐

OFFICIAL STAMPS

Various Stamps of Queen Victoria and King Edward VII Overprinted in Black.

I.R. OFFICIAL (O 1)	I. R. OFFICIAL (O 2)	O. W. OFFICIAL (O 3)
ARMY OFFICIAL (O 4)	ARMY OFFICIAL (O 5)	GOV⊤ PARCELS (O 7)
BOARD OF EDUCATION (O 8)	R.H. OFFICIAL (O 9)	ADMIRALTY OFFICIAL (O 10)

1 Inland Revenue

Overprinted with Types O 1 or O 2 (5s, 10s, £1)

1882–1901 *Queen Victoria*

O 1	52	$\frac{1}{2}$d	green	.. ..	10·00	3·00	☐ ☐
O 5		$\frac{1}{2}$d	blue	..	25·00	15·00	☐ ☐
O13	67	$\frac{1}{2}$d	vermilion	..	1·10	40	☐ ☐
O17		$\frac{1}{2}$d	green	..	3·00	2·25	☐ ☐
O 3	57	1d	lilac (Die II)	..	1·00	65	☐ ☐
O 6	64	$2\frac{1}{2}$d	lilac	..	£110	35·00	☐ ☐
O14	70	$2\frac{1}{2}$d	purple on blue		50·00	4·00	☐ ☐
O 4	43	6d	grey (Plate 18) .		75·00	20·00	☐ ☐
O18	75	6d	purple on red	..	£100	20·00	☐ ☐
O 7	65	1s	green	.. ..	£2500	£450	☐ ☐
O15	78	1s	green	.. ..	£200	20·00	☐ ☐
O19		1s	green and red .		£600	£100	☐ ☐
O 9	59	5s	red ..	..	£1300	£400	☐ ☐
O10	60	10s	blue	..	£2250	£475	☐ ☐
O11	61	£1	brown (Wmk Crowns) ..	..	£18000		☐ ☐
O12		£1	brown (Wmk Orbs)	..	£27000		☐ ☐
O16		£1	green	.. ..	£3500	£450	☐ ☐

1902–04 *King Edward VII*

O20	79	½d blue-green	..	15·00	1·50	□	□
O21		1d red	..	10·00	70	□	□
O22	82	2½d blue	.. ..	£400	60·00	□	□
O23	79	6d purple	..	£85000	£65000	□	□
O24	89	1s green and red	..	£500	65·00	□	□
O25	91	5s red	..	£4000	£1300	□	□
O26	92	10s blue	..	£15000	£9500	□	□
O27	93	£1 green	..	£12000	£6000	□	□

2 Office of Works

Overprinted with Type O 3

1896–1902 *Queen Victoria*

O31	67	½d vermilion	..	90·00	40·00	□	□
O32		½d green	..	£150	75·00	□	□
O33	57	1d lilac (Die II)		£150	40·00	□	□
O34	74	5d dull pur & bl		£750	£150	□	□
O35	77	10d dull pur & red	..	£950	£225	□	□

1902–03 *King Edward VII*

O36	79	½d blue-green	..	£350	80·00	□	□
O37		1d red ..	..	£350	80·00	□	□
O38	81	2d green and red	..	£600	75·00	□	□
O39	82	2½d blue		£700	£200	□	□
O40	88	10d purple and red		£5000	£1500	□	□

3 Army

Overprinted with Types O 4 (½d, 1d) or O 5 (2½d, 6d)

1896–1901 *Queen Victoria*

O41	67	½d vermilion	..	1·10	50	□	□
O42		½d green	..	1·75	3·00	□	□
O43	57	1d lilac (Die II)		1·00	50	□	□
O44	70	2½d purple on blue		4·00	2·00	□	□
O45	75	6d purple on red	..	13·00	8·00	□	□

Overprinted with Type O 4

1902 *King Edward VII*

O48	79	½d blue-green	..	1·75	65	□	□
O49		1d red		1·25	55	□	□
O50		6d purple	..	60·00	30·00	□	□

4 Government Parcels

Overprinted with Type O 7

1883–1900 *Queen Victoria*

O69	57	1d lilac (Die II)	..	25·00	8·00	□	□
O61	62	1½d lilac	.. ..	£100	25·00	□	□
O65	68	1½d purple and green		12·00	2·00	□	□
O70	69	2d green and red	..	45·00	7·00	□	□
O71	73	4½d green and red	..	£100	75·00	□	□
O62	63	6d green	..	£750	£275	□	□
O66	75	6d purple on red	..	25·00	10·00	□	□
O63	64	9d green	..	£625	£175	□	□
O67	76	9d purple and blue		55·00	15·00	□	□
O64	44	1s brown (Plate 13)		£425	70·00	□	□
O64*c*		1s brown (Plate 14)		£725	£110	□	□
O68	78	1s green	..	£120	70·00	□	□
O72		1s green and red	..	£160	50·00	□	□

1902 *King Edward VII*

O74	79	1d red ..	..	15·00	5·00	□	□
O75	81	2d green and red	..	65·00	15·00	□	□
O76	79	6d purple	..	£100	15·00	□	□
O77	87	9d purple and blue		£225	50·00	□	□
O78	89	1s green and red	..	£350	85·00	□	□

5 Board of Education

Overprinted with Type O 8

1902 *Queen Victoria*

O81	74	5d dull pur & bl	..	£500	£100	□	□
O82	78	1s green and red	..	£950	£375	□	□

1902–04 *King Edward VII*

O83	79	½d blue-green	..	16·00	7·00	□	□
O84		1d red ..	..	16·00	6·00	□	□
O85	82	2½d blue	..	£500	50·00	□	□
O86	85	5d purple and blue		£2000	£950	□	□
O87	89	1s green and red	..	£35000	£25000	□	□

6 Royal Household

Overprinted with Type O 9

1902 *King Edward VII*

O91	79	½d blue-green	..	£150	95·00	□	□
O92		1d red ..		£130	85·00	□	□

7 Admiralty

Overprinted with Type O 10

1903 *King Edward VII*

O101	79	½d blue-green	..	9·00	3·00	□	□
O102		1d red ..	..	5·00	2·50	□	□
O103	80	1½d purple and green		60·00	40·00	□	□
O104	81	2d green and red	..	£100	50·00	□	□
O105	82	2½d blue	..	£120	40·00	□	□
O106	83	3d purple on yellow		£100	35·00	□	□

> **Minimum Price.** The minimum price quoted is 10p. This represents a handling charge rather than a basis for valuing common stamps. Where the actual value of a stamp is less than 10p this may be apparent when set prices are shown, particularly for sets including a number of 10p stamps. It therefore follows that in valuing common stamps the 10p catalogue price should not be reckoned automatically since it covers a variation in real scarcity.

The British Philatelic Bulletin is the Post Office's monthly magazine for stamp collectors.

* First with the news on forthcoming GB stamps
* Authorative articles on past issues, postal history and thematic collecting
* Full colour throughout on fine art paper
* Convenient compact format
* Great value for money – just 50p a month (UK)

Available on subscription from:

British Philatelic Bureau
Freepost
20 Brandon Street
EDINBURGH EH3 0HN

Rates current at November, 1990:

UK and Europe £6 per year
Rest of the World airmail £9.25

The Post Office also publishes the fortnightly *British Postmark Bulletin* **for collectors of special handstamps and postmark slogans. Subscription details are available on request.**

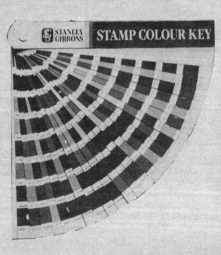

YOU CANNOT AFFORD
TO MISS OUR FREE ILLUSTRATED GB LIST
chock-full of both straightforward and specialised material

FOR THE "GB SPECIALIST"

1. SELECTED ITEMS SECTION

For the connoisseur and specialist who collects items of quality and rarity. Line Engraved with scarcer Plates and Maltese Crosses, Surface Printed cds used and with Edward VII & George V shades with Certificates.

FOR "THE COLLECTOR OF G.B."

2. BARGAINS SECTION

Full of hundreds of inexpensive items from a few pounds upwards. Very strong in Line Engraved, Surface Printed & KEVII, from fillers at only 2% of Cat. to fine mint & VFU singles. Lots of unusual pmks, Used Abroad, KGV shades through to QEII Commems.

Whether average or specialist collector, you cannot afford to miss our free list – so write today!

GB POSTAL AUCTION

Our regular GB-only Postal Auction provides the collector with the opportunity to purchase at 'dealer prices'. From Postal History through to QEII varieties, from basic stamps through to major rarities.

FREE CATALOGUE FOR OUR NEXT SALE – AVAILABLE NOW!

WE URGENTLY NEED TO BUY

Fine quality and rare items/collections of Great Britain.
To get the best price it always pays to contact the specialists first,
so contact Barry Fitzgerald at 'The Embassy' Today.

WANTS LISTS … WANTS LISTS … WANTS LISTS …
We constantly supply medium to rare items to clients whose collections range from average to Gold Medal standard – so make sure we are aware of you, and whatever your G.B. requirements may be.

Embassy Philatelists

MANFIELD HOUSE, (7th Floor)
376 THE STRAND, LONDON WC2R 0LR
Tel: 071-240 1527. Fax: 071-497 3623 VAT No 228 8653 31

FREE STAMPS!

YOUR INVITATION ...

Complete below to receive a PERSONALISED selection of our GB approvals. **NO OBLIGATION** and new applicants will be offered **£10-worth FREE.***

(Full details with 1st selection)

❶ Tick: GB ☐   Channel I ☐   IOM ☐

❷ We supply ALL the British Commonwealth as well. If you want approvals from any Br. C/Wlth country just add the names here: _____

_____

❸ Tick periods of interest:
All Reigns ☐   (or)
QV ☐   EDVII ☐   GV ☐   GVI ☐
QEII–1970 ☐   QEII–1971–date ☐

❹ Tick conditions:
Mint and used ☐   Used only ☐
Mint only ☐   U/M only ☐

❺ Tick price range per stamp/set:
to £5 ☐   to £10 ☐   to £25 ☐   to £50 + ☐

❻ Your name, address and phone No:

_____

_____

_____

❼ A reference (or a credit card number):

_____

YES! Please send selections of approvals tailor-made to my specifications above. I will return if not required and pay for those kept within 10 days. **As a new client I claim £10-worth FREE as offered.** I may cancel at any time.
ALL APPROVALS SUBJECT TO STANDARD CONDITIONS SENT WITH EACH SELECTION.
Under 18's – parents please sign.

Signed: **Date:**

C
B **LOOK – NO envelope or stamp needed!**
S Simply cut out this page, fold in half as shown, tape edge and post **FREEPOST!**

If you'd rather not cut this catalogue, please apply by letter/FAX (or telephone if you have a credit card) or see our full page advert in your stamp magazine.

SUPERB SELECTIONS

View in your own home!

★ **Superior approvals service.** More and more collectors find the R. Warren way the best way to expand their GB collection.

★ **Convenient home approvals** when YOU want them. Inspect, consider, choose – from the **comfort of home**. NO OBLIGATION, NO PRESSURE.

★ **Huge stocks.** Nearly every stamp listed in this catalogue is ALWAYS in stock – mint and used. From the cheapest to the rarest. And all available to look at **BEFORE** you buy.

★ **Keen prices always.** From 1/20th or less of the catalogue value!

★ **Members PTS and UDPA** Years of experience and hundreds and hundreds of customers ensure your satisfaction. Customers order our approvals again and again!

★ **UK's NUMBER ONE approvals service.** Fill in this form to find out why. APPLY TODAY!

CASH WAITING FOR YOU! If it's British, or British Commonwealth, and worth £250 or more, then we're buyers! TOP PRICES PAID FOR ALL BRITISH STAMPS.

NO STAMP REQUIRED IN U.K.

R. Warren
FREEPOST
Lingfield
Surrey RH7 6ZA
England

Tel: 0342 833413
Fax: 0342 833892

Lightly sellotape this edge